Praise for
No Ordinary Men

Using as his baseline and touchstone the classic fantasy *The Wizard of Oz*, pastor Bryan Salminen takes males who are interested in becoming truly human and truly masculine on a journey to fulfillment with the Incarnate Christ—the One who "has come to us in the freedom of love, not needing to experience our humanity and masculinity but freely choosing to do so out of love" (p. 185). This is not watered-down stuff. Pastor Salminen unfolds a true theology of the cross, centered in a God who is willing to pay a costly price "to love us into life" (p. 186). All bases are covered, including career, fatherhood, sexuality and marriage, and pain and emotions. Read this book if you want to know the truth about yourself and about your Savior God.

Dr. James W. Voelz

Bryan Salminen's book, *No Ordinary Men*, provides a most illuminating look *into* men who live as fathers, husbands, brothers, and friends—men in relationships—men and their families. He takes the unique perspective of organizing his book around the characters and story of *The Wizard of Oz*.

The characters and their personalities are symbolic of different traits that characterize so many modern men. For example, in the chapter "The Scarecrow," Salminen describes men "whose heads are filled with straw." That is, they "have no brains when it comes to relationships." They can't figure out what their family needs from them emotionally. They have been taught that they are supposed to think, solve problems, analyze. They don't understand the importance of emotions and tenderness.

In "The Cowardly Lion," Salminen gives the reader a stark description of "the cowardly male." His observations are especially penetrating. On the outside, many men present an image of strength and toughness. But inside, they are nothing but cowards. They fear commitment. They fear emotions. They fear intimacy. Salminen exposes many so-called "macho men" for what they really are—cowards. They don't admit it. They don't frame their behavior in these terms. And, in fact, they often justify their cowardly behavior as "an act of courage." But after reading this chapter, they would have a hard time denying the simple truth.

Salminen is a heart surgeon. He works on peoples' hearts. And so, like a surgeon's scalpel, the book is designed to cut to the hearts of men who may not realize how sick they really are. Like any good surgery, the operation is painful and humbling, but also quite necessary. With his scalpel, Salminen peels away the layers of self-justification, denial, myth-making, and all the other defense mechanisms which men use to justify their behavior, and he exposes the sinful heart for what it is—a painful and humbling process indeed. This book will force many men to look at themselves in a way that they never have before, and many will not at all like what they see.

In joyful and uplifting prose, Salminen proclaims Christ to the man with heart trouble. The power of the book is not in the information it conveys. It is not that after reading it, a man knows just what he must do "to change for the better." No, much more than that, the power of the book is in what the book *does*. By humbling and then restoring, by killing and then making alive, *No Ordinary Men* itself changes you.

A man cannot thoughtfully read this book and come away unaffected. Indeed, many, I believe, will come away rightfully humbled, but at the same time with a new strength and energy and with new hope for their closest relationships. After reading it, many men will look at themselves honestly for the first time in a long time, and—while frightened by what they see—also find comfort and hope from one totally outside themselves who loves them and has redeemed them, sick heart and all.

Salminen has done the job of a master heart surgeon. Hopefully, Bible study groups and men's groups of all kinds will take advantage of this therapy. If they do, I am sure that many will "live" because of his skill, and many relationships will be saved as a result.

Dr. Timothy E. Saleska

no ordinary men

REVISED EDITION

BRYAN R. SALMINEN, Ph.D.

N

drsal@new-gate.org

Published by New-gate, Inc.
www.new-gate.org

A No Ordinary Christian Book
www.noordinarychristian.com

ISBN: 978-0-9801973-0-3

All New-gate, Inc., Full Contact Rules, Real Life Rules, and No Ordinary Christian Products are available at special discounts for bulk purchases and charitable organizations. Please visit www.new-gate.org for additional information.

Men-Psychology. Men-Religious life. Masculinity. Masculinity-Religious aspects-Christianity.

Printed in the United States of America

0 9 8 7 6 5 4 3 2 1

To my beloved wife
who continually forgives me,
at times, a very ordinary man

And my daughter Lauren,
and sons, David, and Michael,
extraordinary children
Gifts of God generously given.

Contents

PREFACE TO REVISED EDITION

Since the publishing of the first edition of ***No Ordinary Men***, I have experienced an enormous amount of changes and challenges. Shortly after the first edition came out, my beloved father contracted terminal cancer and was gone within a few short months. However, he left this world for the mansions of paradise as we all need to leave: in Christ, in faith, in the forgiveness of his sins. I miss him terribly, but confident in hope that we shall meet again.

Shortly after my father's death, I was elected President of Concordia University, Austin Texas. It was, of course, assumed that I would accept the position as president. I wanted to. I planned on it. My entire career had been preparing me for such a position. The board of regents of the university certainly planned on it. The electors in the Synod did as well. But I was elected on the Tuesday before Thanksgiving and I laid to rest my father's remains on that following Saturday. As I stood over the grave of my father, with the cold November winds whistling around me, I recall looking at my mother and saying to myself, "there is no way I can move another 1,500 miles from her." It seemed impossible at the time to relocate, when I was already feeling so dislocated from home, family, loved ones. Through much tears, grief and anguish of soul, I declined the position. It was a time of testing to be sure and I struggled with enormous regrets and doubts. However, I continued to serve the Lord of the church in St. Louis. It was, to say the least, a transformational time in my life.

And then in the spring of 2005, my own personal "9/11" struck when I left the seminary, for personal reasons, although very painful ones. It is not necessary to go into the details of such a transition, what is vitally important, however, is God's grace and mercy, and healing in Christ Jesus. Sin in your life or mine, is always boring. The Gospel and good news of Christ is new, novel, and thrilling. And I have learned since my departure that despite our own suffering, there is always a bigger picture. While we are called to look suffering full in the face and confront it with courage and compassion, suffering is not to be our master. Whether we are the one in the bed of a nursing home, never to rise again, or the one tending to a loved one wracked with sobs over the loss of a child, or the one suffering due to our sin and failures, our purpose is to still to give glory to God. Yes, we are to fight against suffering, disease, and death, but sometimes they will appear to win. The spirit of the Lord is upon us to bind and heal. However, ultimately the goal is not simply the healing, for even those who experience healing will go on to suffer in yet other ways. We are to heal, bind up, and comfort so that God will be glorified. Whatever the backdrop to a life, my life, honor to the name of Jesus has become my goal.

In the context of trying to understand my own life in light of my own sin and failures, and there are many, I have learned that God uses brokenness. Brokenness does not lead inevitably to uselessness. God is the God of life, the One who redeems. Our faith teaches us that out of suffering, loss, and death, God brings life. No matter the extent of the brokenness, no matter the depths of the pit, the God of the impossible can beautify and use what appears useless to us.

And so today, I write as a broken man; but one who has met the redeemer. He is a man of sorrows and intimate with grief. He was left alone, regarded with contempt. He is scarred for all eternity. His suffering has left its tracks across His face. His hands and feet carry marks of the violence done to Him. He was afflicted, struck, crushed, stripped and oppressed. Suffering does that, you know; it leaves its mark all over those who must endure. And I carry mine.

And so the second edition of this book means a great deal more to me than when it was first published. I am now scarred, war torn, bruised and battered; but also healed. I have seen the work of the redeemer close up. I have watched Him comfort, bind up my wounds, set me free, rebuild and repair. I have seen Him tenderly choose me when I felt rejected, strengthen me when I felt weakest, carry my broken life and heart in his hands.

I have had an enormous privilege of seeing how Christ not only ministers to others, but ministers to me personally. The Gospel has come home "to roost," if you will. And the more I know Him and see His work, the more I become what Amy Carmichael refers to, "As a worshipper at the feet."

I pray that this new edition and the study guide that accompanies it will be an enormous blessing to you. I hope that as you see yourself in these pages, you will realize that like me, you are at times, very ordinary, very sinful, and quite shallow. But you will also see yourselves in the eyes of the redeemer, Christ Jesus, who makes all things new. Because of Christ our Lord and His death and resurrection, we are now His extraordinary men. Unique, unrepeatable miracles of God's grace in Christ.

Bryan R. Salminen

Introduction

Dante said, "In the midst of life I find myself in a dark wood." I only recently find myself emerging from my own dark wood. Throughout my adult life I have had to come to terms with my own masculinity or better, my misunderstanding of masculinity. I have continually attempted to define myself based on the expectations of others. I have repeatedly tried to be something I'm not. The masculine myth, which I will define in this book, narrowed and constricted my life.

I have lived my life trying to please others, hoping thereby to win some approval. Because I have been driven by the goals, dreams, and expectations of others, I have had very little time to "find" me. This realization saddens me. I have looked in the mirror of my own life and have not liked what I've seen. I've seen shallowness, self-centeredness, and a great longing to be loved. It is that longing that has driven me to do and become so many things I despise. Rather than turning to those who have been given to me to love and turning ultimately to my God who loves me in Christ, I have chased after shadows. Sadly, those shadows have come back to haunt me.

Despite my failures in my journey, God is always good. The one constant throughout this sin-filled life of mine has been the God who revealed Himself to me a long, long time ago. In January of 1960, the Lord put me on the journey of my life. It was then that my mother and father brought me to the baptismal font and the Lord said, "This is My beloved Son." Even as God's Spirit hovered over the chaos of the unformed world in the book of Genesis, so God has continually hovered over the chaos of my unformed life. God in Christ claimed me in the baptismal waters and placed His mark upon me. Admittedly, I have forgotten the mark at times. I have lived as if God did not exist. I have kept Him at bay. And yet—there is always with God the "and yet"—God is faithful. God forgives sin. God forgives me. In His forgiveness I began my journey. In His forgiveness I continue my journey. And in His forgiveness my journey will some day come to an end—at least in this world.

But there is a point to this journey. Too many people today discuss life as a journey with no destination. It has become fashionable to pretend that reasonable and educated people could avoid the embarrassment of religion by sticking close to demonstrable facts and testable hypotheses. But people have deluded themselves. Life for so many has become empty, meaningless, "A tale told by an idiot, full of sound and fury signifying nothing."[1] People have reduced life to a story without a point, a process without a purpose, a journey without a goal, an affair without a climax, an accidental collision of mindless atoms. What little wisdom we have salvaged from our overload of facts seems to point us toward despair and nihilism.

But for me and for all those who are "in Christ," our journey ends where it began—with God. We see life differently. We see it from a divine perspective. We view it through the lenses of faith where Jesus Christ is Lord. There is a purpose to my life and yours. There is hope amidst a hopeless and despairing world. And on the journey we make, we never go it alone. Immanuel, God with us, is indeed just that—with us, for us, above us, alongside us.

And God, the giver of all good and perfect gifts, gives us others on the journey as well. We are not alone. For me, the companion of my life who has helped me emerge from the very dark wood has been my beloved wife, Casey. In 1986 she came into my life and I can say with the utmost confidence, life has never been the same. It has not been one blissful event after another. Life has been very difficult for us at various times in our marriage. I have failed her in so many ways. Yet somehow she remains faithful. I still find it incredible—she loves me. She actually loves me with all my imperfections—and there are many. Warts and all, she accepts, loves, and forgives me for my many failures. Much of the "success" of my journey can be attributed to her. When I felt like quitting—on myself and my projects and goals—she encouraged me. She was a believer. She believed in me more than I ever believed in myself.

And as a result, I too became a believer. I began to see myself emerging from the dark wood. I began to recognize what the Lord of my life wanted of me. In Christ, I was a winner. Sinner to be sure, but saint nevertheless. God had redeemed me in His Son and had come to me in holy Baptism, and it was a matter of living out or actualizing the person He had already declared me to be. God set me on the journey. And in a very real sense, God was the one who brought me forth from the darkest of all woods. St. Paul says, "For He has rescued us from the dominion of darkness and brought us into the kingdom of the

Son He loves, in whom we have redemption, the forgiveness of sins" (Colossians 1:13-14). While lost in my own wood of sin and despair, God found me and set me on the path of life.

The journey has been a challenge. It has been filled with wonder and awe. It has at times terrified me. But despite it all, it has been a journey I wouldn't have missed. I have learned much in 47 years. Primarily I've learned about how good God is and how desperately I need His love and mercy. But I've also learned that God has made me His unique, unrepeatable miracle. He won me for Himself. He claimed me to be His own. And He has given me a special song that only I can sing. He has given me a message that only I can deliver. He has given me a heart that can be broken very easily but that can beat with His love for other people.

Something else happened on my journey that has left a lasting impact on me. During the original drafting of this book, my mother-in-law was diagnosed with inoperable cancer. Dorie, much like my own mother, was truly one of God's special moms. With a heart as big as Texas, she had the gift of welcoming everyone into her home and into her heart. She did that with me. When my own mother was five hundred miles away, Dorie provided that place and space which only moms can provide. She didn't know a stranger because she was able to draw even strangers in and make them friends.

But in 1997, she began to die. Leaving our home in Ann Arbor, Michigan, we began a new leg in the journey at our new home in St. Louis, Missouri. We were about ten minutes from my in-laws' home. And then we were jolted by the news: "Dorie has cancer." Jolt doesn't seem strong enough. We were devastated. During the last four months of Dorie's life, my wife was able to take care of her. Along with her dad and sister, Casey was able to spend the last four months of her mom's life doing for her what she had always done for them—show love.

During this time, Casey and her mother had those very important talks we all need to have sometime during our life's journey. They talked of home, of life, of love. They talked about regrets—about wanting to do some things, but never having the time. They talked about victories won, such as our marriage staying together and becoming stronger during turbulent times. Dorie and Don also had been through one tragic accident after another with his job as an air traffic reporter in St. Louis.

But Dorie also fretted about losing some of her mental abilities. She couldn't remember things. The cancer was affecting her long-term and short-term memory. She had always loved life, but did not love or even like the situation she was in. Yet she faced even this most serious of issues with the utmost confidence. During one of those intimate conversations between mother and daughter, Casey asked her, "Mom, are you afraid?" To which Dorie, confident in her baptismal faith, replied, "Of course not, Dear. Jesus is with me." And of course, He was and still is as she is now a member of the Church Triumphant.

Dorie was called to her heavenly home in February 1998. As she wanted it, her family was gathered around, her pastor was there, and she was ushered into the throne room of heaven by God's holy angels. We miss her dearly but rejoice that we will meet again in the mansions of heaven.

Shortly after Dorie's death, I was visiting a local mall. I watched the happy families strolling along, looking at the various items in the stores. I saw young kids and older ones walking by themselves. I saw moms and dads holding hands and bending over in belly laughs. I watched as some parents picked up their children and held them in strong arms of love. So many people seemed connected and happy. I wished they could remain that way forever. I wanted to shout to them, "Love each other while you can!"

Dorie taught us wondrous things, right up to the end. She taught us to love. She would reach forward and pat her grandchildren's faces and say, "I love you." She taught us the value of time. We realize now how precious it is—we don't have forever to show love for one another. Her death also taught us to look and to see ... and that the people we love aren't going to be the same all the time.

And it struck me that we don't look at one another anymore in our world. We're so busy *doing* things that we don't stop to look at one another. We are meant to care for one another. Despite the differences among us—in gender, race, politics, and religion—we are called to love one another. It is the connections among us that are vital to the success of the journey. Like it or not, we need one another. We need to be loved and accepted and we need to connect with other people.

And we need one another because our time is short. Life is fleeting. We need to love one another while we can, because in a moment, in a twinkling of an eye, the one we so long to love is gone. I have seen the beginning of my life cycle and, although I'm only 47, I can see the end of my life cycle as well. Time moves so quickly on the journey and I want to make the most of the moment, the time, the relationships the Lord has given me.

I mention Dorie—her life and her death—because living through the experience of loving, losing, and letting, her go to her heavenly Father has changed me. The entire event has helped me immensely in understanding my own journey—that the stuff of my life and yours is made up of relationships and people. The journey we take is made up of many things, but it seems to me that the most significant events are those involving important people in our lives. E. M. Forster gives us his classic phrase, "Only connect." And so it is that we must make the most of these moments our Lord has given us to connect with one another—not merely ourselves, but our wives, our children, our friends, our family. They not only make the journey with us, they make it worthwhile.

I have attempted in this book to describe the masculine journey. At times, this description is indicative of men in general. At other times, it is interspersed with personal anecdotes and illustrations. I agree with Carl Jung who said, "That which is most personal is most universal." I hope as you read the account of my own journey you might see yourself reflected in the pages. I hope what holds you, if nothing else, is the possibility that somewhere among all those pictures of people you never knew and places you never saw you may come across something or someone you recognize. Who knows, there might even be the possibility that as the pages flip by, on one of them you may catch a glimpse of yourself.

This book also describes the masculine journey from a distinctively Christ-centered perspective. My life is bound up with His. For me, there is no other life or hope than that which is given in the life, death, and resurrection of Jesus Christ. He makes life worth living and makes all things possible—even the trip down a yellow brick road.

Bryan R. Salminen

1 *The Mythical Journey*

A MAN'S QUEST FOR WHOLENESS

Shortly after the meeting the young Tom Corey, Silas Lapham comments, "I could make a man of that fellow if I had him in the business with me. There's stuff in him."[2] To "make a man" of a fellow? Before and during the Civil War, boys seemingly became men simply through the addition of years; but in late nineteenth-century America, men needed "making."

A century later, society talks a great deal about "the American man," as if there was some quality that remained stable over decades, or even within a single decade. Yet many men feel lost as they grope their way through the mythical darkness of "American manhood." Many men find themselves on a journey they had never planned on making and one with no clear destination. The only thing which might be clear to them is that they are making a journey, but one which has been prescribed for them by a "masculine culture" with its own set of rules. The challenge is, of course, discovering the rules and deciding whether one can live with them or live without them.

I speak of journeys because all of us, male and female, are on the journey of our lives. The metaphor of life as a road is an ancient one, and you and I are travelers along that road whether we think of it that way or not, traveling from the unknown into the unknown. For many men, the "masculine journey" has led them down a very rough and dangerous road. The signposts suggest that those who travel the "masculine road" will lack intimate relationships with other men because they have been taught to view them as competitors not to be trusted.

Another signpost suggests that sharing feelings is taboo because sharing will make men vulnerable and, on this journey, one cannot be vulnerable. Men have been led to believe that preparation for the masculine journey requires buying masculine stereotypes which tell them how to think, feel, and behave. These stereotypes depict their character as men within congregations, as leaders in the community, as husbands and fathers. Our culture's concept of masculinity has produced a script that prescribes for men certain ways to think, feel, and behave as men—anything else is viewed as "feminine" and unthinkable.

Men sometimes act as if their lives resemble a car driven down a road with a clearly defined midline: manly behaviors on one side, "sissy" behaviors on the other. This hardly appears to be a formula for a happy, well-balanced life. It's more like a prescription for raising effective workers and warriors, not fathers, husbands, and good friends.

Of course, the real difficulty in giving up this prescription is that it works! There are results. There is success if we follow the script—success narrowly defined to be sure, but success nonetheless. By following the masculine script, men are effective at their jobs, in control, in charge. By following the masculine script, men can run corporate headquarters, governments, banks, and even churches. And, of course, many men think they can also run their families, children, and spouses the same way they do the office.

Changing the Script

However, when it comes to relationships, all bets are off. Who knows what will happen as men leave the office and enter their homes? You can't control and order the family the way you do employees. Somehow, loving relationships don't thrive that way. In fact, they shrivel and wither under that kind of regime. *Regime* may sound strong, but what else can one say about a man who enters his home and begins to bark out orders as if his loved ones were no more than the family pet? And that does happen as many broken homes and relationships will attest.

To change the script, however, requires an incredible amount of energy and even courage for some men. I am convinced that an important part of the male journey requires that we take off our masks. If we really want to change the masculine script and begin a different journey, it requires that we look within. What in the world are we going to find? It may be that we discover we are vulnerable. We'll find doubts, fears, regrets, and worries. We're not perfect. We are not always in control. But the mask of control at least shields us from our own fears, our own lack of control. We are safe. So we continue to wear the masks despite the shallow relationships all around us.

I'll admit that a new and different journey is a bit scary. But at the same time, it is incredibly exciting. There is, in the journey, the possibility of a delicious surprise awaiting us. The undiscovered self can become an unexpected resource. Self-knowledge is empowering.

Nevertheless, there is a pattern deeply rooted in masculine stereotypes that creates inappropriate expectations and blurs our ability to see the possibility of many kinds of journeys. The masculine script is built around the image of a quest, a journey through a timeless landscape toward an end that is specific, though not fully known. In the pursuit of a quest it is essential to resist the transitory contentment of attractive way stations and side roads, in which obstacles are overcome because the goal is visible on the horizon. The end is already apparent in the beginning.

The Model of Manhood

The model of manhood held up for most men is one of early decision and commitment, often to an educational preparation that launches a single rising trajectory. Ambition, we imply, should be focused, and men worry about whether they are defining their goals and making the right decisions early enough to get on track. You go to medical school and this determines later alternatives—whether you choose prosperity in the suburbs or the more dramatic and exceptional life of discovery and dedication. Graduation is supposed to be followed by the first real job, representing a step on an ascending ladder.

We don't expect long answers when we ask children what they want to be when they grow up, any more than we expect a list of names in response to questions about marriage. But we have reduced manhood to entrance into a fully rational existence, implying that reason is all that matters in terms of growth and potential. This tendency also suggests there is some fixed point in time where one finally "arrives" and is introduced into this full state of manhood.

Much of the current literature on men's issues suggests that men in our culture are in the middle of a deep dilemma. They are the most externally powerful group of people in the world; they know the formula for success; they are privy to the old boys' club; they have all the advantages of strength and skill; they make more money than women; they have visibility. At the same time many of them feel trapped in their roles, with very few other options in life, having to compete forever to get to the glorified "top." They are very unhappy. The dilemma is that they can't figure out *why* they're unhappy. They have or are headed for all the things society has promised men who do well. Yet something is wrong, and they're unclear what it is. And no one feels sorry for them because, after all, they're on top and they should be happy. So characteristically they twist and turn, and about the time of midlife show their deep-seated dilemma by leaving their wives, losing their jobs, moving away, pretending to be twenty-five again, getting ill, being miserable, or dying.

The problem is that the dream they all thought they had bought into freely is a myth. They are in much more tightly prescribed boxes than most women are, and they don't know how to get out. The prescription for men is to get education or skills to land a job at twenty, work with few breaks until sixty-five, and then die within five years. They look at the dream: the right position with the responsibility and authority and power, the right salary the right home in the right place, the right spouse, and the right kids. And somewhere along the way they discover (or more accurately, try to hide) that they either do not really want or cannot achieve the dream their family, peers, community, and they themselves have fostered. So they feel like failures because they are not perfect. And, of course, this is the first big part of the myth. It says that perfection is desirable and that men can surely attain it because of all their opportunities. The second and equally big part of the myth says that being perfect means meeting our culture's definition of "success" which will bring satisfaction, happiness, or some reward.

So what do most men do? Most men who face this dilemma just take a peek at it and find it too awesome to investigate. They close off the part of themselves that is beginning to ask questions—the part getting suffocated in the narrow box—and they plod along, complaining of "something wrong in the organization" or of their inability to change because they've got too much invested already. To look at the unknown and to sort out and unravel the long-term myths with which they have learned to operate is just too frightening and confusing. Our culture also prescribes men's behavior and emotions. They are to be characteristically strong and not show emotion. Looking at the dilemma and the myths would force them to look at their real selves, their inner life, perhaps even to feel some new emotions, and that is both unusual and frightening.

What's at Stake?

It is one thing for me to explain to men that succeeding externally is not enough and that men in our culture may have to move beyond the traditional expectations they have of themselves; it is quite another thing to be a man in the position of wondering whether, in considering another way of being, he will lose all he has gained, or lose what it means, in his mind, to be a male. For most men, to be male is to be powerful, to have the success and symbols of power. That power is synonymous with men; it seems that power was and is in fact a way to describe men, and to consider taking it away from them is to ask them to give up their primary identity and search for another. As we all know any change is difficult. It implies giving up something, a difficult task even for the strongest.

These assumptions of one single journey that leads to the "full state of manhood" are no longer valid. The evidence is everywhere. Men recognize the shallowness and loneliness of following the masculine script. Men have seen relationships squandered because they refused to change and become more than they were. Men have discovered that the masculine journey leads to lives devoid of significant, lasting, meaningful relationships. And most important, there always seems to be "something missing." Men find themselves in exile—from family, love, home, themselves. Questions seem to haunt men who allow themselves to ponder: Why are we so restless, so anxious? Why are we so hollowed out by longing and etched by the acid of loneliness when we have our wives, children, dogs, cats, and careers? Is there some ecstasy, some divine madness, some overpowering enthusiasm that would sweep us away and purge the timidity and fear that haunts our entire existence?

The common cry from men in need of help is, “I know there is something more to my life, but I just don’t know what it is. It's too hard and scary to change.”

The Analogy

It is time to explore a different journey, not one which leads to the mythical qualities of "the real man," but one which leads us to being "real people." And the classic story *The Wizard of Oz* provides the framework for helping us discover and uncover our real identity as men.

Caught up in the Kansas cyclone, a child named Dorothy is blown away to the Land of Oz, which is a strange and beautiful place but which she knows she must leave to return to her home in Kansas. The only one who can help her return is the great Wizard of Oz himself, so she sets off for the Emerald City to find him. On her way, she is joined by three remarkable creatures, each of whom has his own favor to ask of the Wizard. The first is a Scarecrow who wants a brain more than anything else. The second is a Tin woodman, who yearns for a heart. The third is a Cowardly Lion, who is searching, of course, for courage. I will not try to describe all the things that happen on their journey except to say that in the manner of fairy tales, most of them are pretty hair-raising, yet somehow the adventurers finally come through. But how?

Their success is rather unexpected, really. For instance, whenever they are confronted with some sort of physical danger, it is the Cowardly Lion who somehow manages to fight their way out of it. Whenever the obstacle is of a more cerebral nature, it is the brainless Scarecrow who figures out a way to circumvent it. And as for the Tin Woodman, who is journeying in search of a heart, although he lends a hand whenever he can, very often he tends to be more of a hindrance than a help because he is so given to being moved by the plight of others that everyone has to rally around him with an oil can to make sure his tears do not rust him. The climax of the tale occurs when, upon reaching the Emerald City at last, they make the shattering discovery that the Great Wizard is not really great at all, not really even a wizard. He is a rather helpless little man with a bald head who says himself that he is a humbug and that he cannot possibly grant the requests of this little band that has journeyed to him from afar. But is this entirely true? Is he really a humbug? Is he really unable to givc them what they want?

The Wizard points out that each of them already has what he traveled such a distance to find. And here we have to listen carefully, because here the fairy tale becomes something more than fantasy, and the journey down the yellow brick road becomes a journey of more than just a Cowardly Lion, a Tin Woodman, and a Scarecrow. Because what the helpless little man who is not and yet really is a wizard says to them is, in effect, that things like a brain, a heart, and courage are never had as gifts, but are always earned.

This seems so obvious that we would think one would have to be a scarecrow not to see it, but that is not so. We men want very much what these three wanted, and that is to become fully men, to become fully persons. And we want it for the same reasons they wanted it: because as things stand now, we know that we are only partly men, partly persons. Like them, we expect that what we want will simply *happen* to us one day, by some sort of wizardry. We tend to say something like this: "I am not now altogether the person I wish I were—my heart is less than a man's heart should be, all shut off behind tin; my brain is a thing stuffed full of the straw of other people's ideas; and courage? There are times when I don't even have the courage to face myself. I am not the man I would like to be, but someday I will become that man. When things straighten out. When all the pressures on me let up a little. When I grow up." But the hard truth is that this day may never come, and for many it has never come simply because they did not understand that courage is his who with his scalp cold with fear acts courageously. A brain—a real brain—is his who knows that he is as much a fool as a scarecrow yet manages somehow to do all that a scarecrow can. A heart is his who is willing to let it be broken. And for all of us men, the one who confronts us with ourselves and with this truth is not a wizard who is a humbug, but God who is a child.

As for the little girl Dorothy, she's infuriated that the Wizard hasn't lived up to his promise and she scolds him: "You're a bad man." And Dorothy's words echo the refrain of so many sons and daughters whose hearts have been broken by their fathers' inability to keep promises.

The Wizard, though (probably because he is a wizard), stands his ground: "No," he explains, "I'm a good man, just a bad wizard."

And how many of us feel that way? We need to help men become good men and forgive them for being bad wizards. We need to help men begin the journey down the yellow brick road to a land of hopefulness and deep, meaningful relationships. During the journey, we need to help men recognize the signposts that direct them to the Emerald City, warning them of dangerous side roads along the way. Most of all, we need to help men understand that there is a great "Wizard," not one who rules Oz, but who rules heaven and earth. Rather than try to be "like gods" as Adam did, we simply have to be what we have been called to be: "a royal priesthood, a holy nation, a people belonging to God, that you may declare the praises of Him who called you out of darkness into His wonderful light" (1 Peter 2:9).

There is another "Wizard," much greater than the Wizard of Oz ever imagined, who has so many delightful surprises for all of us. Jesus, a longtime ago, looked at twelve men He had called to be His disciples and said to them, "You are the light of the world, the salt of the earth" (see Matthew 5:13-16). Though weak-kneed and cowardly, sometimes lacking any kind of hearts at all, never once understanding a word He had to say, these scarecrows, tin men, and cowardly lions were called to be God's saints, forgiven sinners, life-givers themselves. With His own "X-ray vision," Jesus not only saw something in them they could never see themselves, He also gave them something they could never earn themselves: new hearts, new brains, new courage for the journey ahead of them. The journey was long. The journey was filled with danger. The journey took them to countries they had never dreamed of. But during the journey, Immanuel was God with them and for them.

And so He is today. Apart from this great "Wizard," we men and women will be forever in exile—wandering, restless, homesick. Only in Him can we "live and move and have our being" writes the author of the books of Acts (17:28). So in Him and in His name we begin our journey.

2 *We're Off to See the Wizard*

GROWING UP MALE

What do you want to be when you grow up? It's not just another question. For men, it's the great question. In fact, it is the question moms and dads, friends, relatives, grandparents, and everyone else who had any concern about you when you were younger asked. In high schools around the country coaches ask their male athletes, "What do you want to be when you grow up?" And of course, the answer some young men might give, "Oh, I want to keep a diary explore the woods, sleep under the stars, and read poetry," is not sufficient. Implied in the very question itself is the answer —you better have a clearly defined goal. And for most men the answer is: go to college, get a job, get married, have kids, get a nice home and then keep getting nicer, bigger, and better homes, cars, and things. Growing up male for most means coming to a point in life where you can say, "There. I have arrived."

I would suggest, however, that "What do you want to be when you grow up?" is not just a question for youth. All of us revisit this question of growth. What do you and I want to be when we "grow up"? I have been serving as a pastor for twenty years, a professor for thirteen years, and a marriage and family therapist for eighteen years, and I still believe the question is important and needs to be kept wide open.

Something in us rears back in indignation, of course. We are not children anymore, most of us. Surely we have our growing up behind us. We have come many a long mile and thought many a long thought. We have taken on serious responsibilities, made hard decisions, weathered many a crisis. Surely the question is, rather: "What are you now and how well are you doing it?" Whatever we are—doctors, lawyers, merchant chiefs, computer analysts, businessmen, school teachers, artists, poets, pastors even—we like to think that one way or another we have already made our mark on the world. We don't even have to ask the question any longer because, for better or for worse, the die has already been cast. Now we simply get on with the game, whatever is left of it for us. That's what life is all about from here on out.

Living the Question

A poet once said, "Live the question." I'm afraid, however, that most people refuse even to *ask* the question, whatever the question might be. Men are taught from early on that life is to be figured out and decided about, not pondered over. Men are also taught early on to be in control. This gets played out in competition with siblings, fights on the block, in sports, and in school. The message is clear that if men are the best at whatever they do, they will be respected and, in turn, will have control over others. They hear this message throughout their lives, and it continues to haunt them until they die. The irony is that the things they have managed to master, control, or accumulate do little to give them the satisfaction they were told to expect. We all know of people who are the best at what they do but still find themselves unsatisfied with life.

These people have been accumulating things they were told would bring them lasting peace and happiness. And they found these things did, in fact, bring them satisfaction, but not all they had hoped for. Usually, these things or accomplishments bring satisfaction for short periods of time. Thus men find it necessary to reach for more in hopes they'll get back the feeling of accomplishment, satisfaction, and control.

Men are driven to be in control of their lives and the lives of those around them. They want assurances that they will be able to determine their fate and, most important, that they will avoid pain from outside forces. They understand at a cognitive level that this is impossible because they see people of great power, wealth, and status experiencing pain and anguish. Take the Kennedy family for example. They are powerful and wealthy, and have lived through incredible tragedy. Yet they work hard to get more control so everything will be all right. Of course, the real issue or question for men is their fundamental fear of not being important, cared for, and useful to others. These emotional needs far outweigh their intellectual understanding of their folly.

The masculine myth drives men to prove that they really are important, loved, and valuable. And men believe it is their responsibility to prove to the world they are worthwhile. I believe this is also the very thing that drives a wedge between men and developing lasting, meaningful relationships with other men. They turn themselves against those who are not able to "suck it up and be a man." And when viewing other men who show signs of vulnerability, or—gasp—emotionality, they treat them as less worthy, the basis of prejudice of all sorts. Many men believe that the more they own, the higher they can climb, the more money they can make, the more control they have. They believe that going to the right schools and achieving the right degrees somehow qualifies them as more "manly" or more successful. And they want these external things because without them they believe they will not be accepted and respected; thereforc, they will be nothing.

If there are any questions to be asked, they are to be asked and answered quickly. To sit and think, daydream, ponder, and wonder is considered a frivolous waste of time. I have come to believe, however, that to "live the question" means to be open to all the possibilities that await. It is essential to live your life in wonder. There is enchantment all around us and we so often let it go by. Living the question means wondering about what your life is, where it will go, and who will go with you. Living the question means pondering the doubts, uncertainties, and vagaries of life. Living the question provides an opportunity for growth, for newness, for something surprising to occur in life. Each person's question is different—and I'm not even sure what my own question is, but I believe it has something to do with the price of being human. How much does a tin man have to pay for a heart? How much does a cowardly lion have to fork over for courage? What does it cost a scarecrow to be a man? Good teacher, what must I do to inherit eternal life? These are the questions of life—eternal life as well. These are the questions that lead to possibilities—to become what God in His mercy and grace has always intended us to become. And who knows, maybe, just maybe, we can be more than we ever dreamed possible.

Becoming

Possibility draws and it also repels. *Becoming* terrifies people. It is the Velveteen Rabbit with his fur all rubbed off. At one point in that story there is an intriguing discussion between a toy rabbit and a toy horse. The toy horse's description of a love relationship is powerful and compelling:

> *"Real isn't how you are made," said the Skin Horse. "It's a thing that happens to you. When a child loves you for a long, long time, not just to play with, but REALLY loves you, then you become Real."*
>
> *"Does it hurt?" asked the Rabbit.*
>
> *"Sometimes," said the Skin Horse, for he was always truthful. "When you are Real you don't mind being hurt."*
>
> *"Does it happen all at once, like being wound up," he asked, "or bit by bit?"*
>
> *"It doesn't happen all at once," said the Skin Horse. "You become. It takes a long time. That's why it doesn't often happen to people who break easily, or have sharp edges, or who have to be carefully kept. Generally, by the time you are Real, most of your hair has been loved off, and your eyes drop out and you get loose in the joints and very shabby. But these things don't matter at all, because once you are Real you can't be ugly, except to people who don't understand."*[3]

Becoming real—that is, loved—is sometimes painful. Becoming fully human is a tear-filled process. And yet, once a person *becomes*, once a person is real, he is no longer ugly! All that matters is that you are real, genuine, authentic. It is this genuineness and authenticity men need to focus on. Growing up male is a script determined by others that one size should fit all. The world tells us what we are to be and shapes us by the end it sets before us. To men, it says work is of primary importance. To women, it says appearance is critical. So both men and women end up with gifts and talents that are unused and unappreciated. Men and women are taught from early on to deny their true selves and assume false selves to please others.

The Rules Have Changed

All men are products of their times. The rules for men have changed a great deal since the 1950s when, to be a man, one was to stay sober, earn a living, remain faithful to his wife, and not beat the kids. Men weren't expected to be emotional, to show affection, to cry to hug or kiss their daughters, and certainly not their sons. Emotions were relegated to the domain of women and no male dared trespass. In fact, emotions were and still are considered "dangerous" for many men. Emotions can't be controlled. They just *are* and if a man allows himself to feel, then who knows what might happen. Better keep one's feelings in check and emotions at a distance. Every young boy knows the ecstasy of feeling great joy and deep sorrow—these emotions give a certain panache to life. But growing up male means growing away from childhood. Growing up male means leaving the world of wonder and tears behind and heading into a brave new world where career, ambition, and tough-mindedness rule.

The Making of a Man

As a child I was always fascinated by stories, myths, fairy tales, and legends. They were the "stuff" of my existence. They enchanted me and helped make life itself seem enchanted. But long ago, when I played with toys, I learned quickly what growing up male meant. It meant saying good-bye to that kind of world. It meant that I had to let go of my wondering, my daydreaming, my pondering, my fantasizing. If I was to be a man, it meant making a name for myself and there were prescribed ways to do that. To sit around and allow words and tales of great heroism to fill my head simply meant my head was being filled with straw.

> *Mrs. Osborn's ninth-grade classroom always seemed dark, but on this particular day it was more depressing than usual. For an eternal afternoon, I sat practicing my grammar exercises, listening to Mrs. Osborn's monotone: "Diagram this sentence and make sure you can put the noun, subject, and verb in their correct place and order. Now repeat and diagram this sentence." Caught somewhere between boredom and despair, I struggled against tears and settled in to wait for the resurrection: the 3:00 bell.*
>
> *And then it happened. A movement outside the window caught my eye and there, in the sweet and redeeming light of the springtime world, was a robin—our state bird—building a nest. Caught in wonder, I followed the progress*

of the nest construction and dreamt of the time when I too would be constructing great things—not nests, but dreams and visions for other people. My diagramming was forgotten until Mrs. Osborn materialized over my shoulder and demanded to how why my page was empty. Instinct warned me that no robin redbreast, no private fascination could provide an excuse for the neglect of my serious educational duties. So I bit my tongue, cherished my wonder in silence, and stayed after school to make up my lesson.

Mrs. Osborn, along with a few of my coaches in high school won more than the day. They won a life. Somehow, someway, they, along with many other authority figures in my life, led me to believe that one plus one is more important than the kind of dreams and visions and wonderings one might have or want to have. Private enthusiasm and passion for life became secondary to achieving clear-cut goals.

It is not surprising that when I finally left the classroom, having achieved two master's degrees and a Ph.D., I could conjugate verbs and analyze syntax. But the little bird was gone. I emerged from graduate school to discover that I was empty of enthusiasm. I had a profession but nothing to profess, knowledge but no wisdom, ideas but few feelings. Rich in techniques but poor in convictions, I had received an education but lost an identity. As I shifted my vocation from student concerned with possessing and organizing ideas to man in search of the wisdom necessary for living vividly, I came to focus on questions I had not been trained to consider, to cherish abilities which had not been cultivated, and to explore feelings which had long remained dormant.

In all fairness to Mrs. Osborn and many like her, she was simply following a prescribed curriculum and a prescribed way of understanding what growing up really meant. Growing up meant growing away from the inner journey and stepping forward to begin a journey that was as clearly marked out for me as the nose on my face. And, as if her life depended on it, she was determined to teach me her lay of the land.

And then there was Coach Gonzales—a good and decent man in so many ways, a man whom I dearly love and respect. But he, like Mrs. Osborn, had been inculcated into a way of believing boys should be men. If there was one thing he hammered into us ninth-grade boys on the freshman basketball team, it was to be men: "Act like a man, a big man, a real man, a macho man." Drill after drill he drove into us that we were to be made of stuff tougher than nails. He would not tolerate any type of pain, tears, or emotional outbursts from his players. Men simply didn't act that way. To win ball games, I suppose, he was right. He was the coach and it was his job to teach us how to win. But he did more than teach us how to play ball and win—he taught us how to be men. He taught us that anyone who even remotely began to show a trace of the "feminine" was inferior. We lived under constant dread of being labeled a sissy, a weakling, a wimp, a queer. We needed to prove ourselves by establishing mastery on the gym floor or with the better-looking girls in our school. But the one thing we never learned was to maneuver the intricacies of relationships with empathy, flexibility, patience, and negotiation. That was the realm of women. From the moment we stepped onto the basketball court, Coach Gonzales meant to shape us into men. He pounded any "sissiness" out of us.

My masculine self-image rested on the assumption that I was somehow intrinsically more masculine than boys who did not wear the basketball uniform. I was prejudiced, not only against boys who were less agile, but against a part of myself. I believed that if I did not compete and succeed, I was not as masculine as I should be. Too few baskets, too many bad passes, meant something was wrong with me. If I was not proficient at basketball, I was not proficient at being a man.

What made matters worse was that no matter how well I did, it was seldom good enough. When I made the freshman basketball team, the boys who had been cut envied me. But what obsessed me was that I was only on the second string and Robby Gregory was the first string center. Even when I won my letter as a sophomore, my self-doubts were not stilled. My letter was for tennis, after all, which was not a contact sport.

To acquire my good self-image, then, I sacrificed an inner freedom that would take years even to begin to recover. I forfeited the freedom not to compete. I absorbed the insidious notion that to compete is manly, and to win more manly still. I learned to measure other boys, and myself, against a standard of masculinity that omitted many of the most vital qualities a man can possess. I became obsessed with developing the parts of myself included in this standard. And I neglected, or actively suppressed, other sides of my personality because they were not part of this arbitrary sexual accounting.

A New Game

Like all but a handful of men, I did not become a professional athlete. The day came when the balls were put away, when the tennis tournaments were over, when the buzzer no longer sounded. The sports mania of adolescence was behind me. I had become a man with a job and a family. My letters, medals, and trophies were—and still are—in Mom and Dad's basement. Competition did not solve marital tensions. Slam-dunks did not impress a crying child. It was definitely a new game I was playing. Except that it was no longer a game, it was life itself. I was no longer a boy trying to be like Michael Jordan; I was a man trying to raise my sons and daughters to be like ... like whom?

> *During one evening practice a teammate broke a leg during a particular drill. Lying on the field in incredible pain, he screamed and cried out for help. Coach, along with many of the other ball players, thought he was overreacting and playing on the sympathies of the coaches and his teammates. Coach ran up to the young man who was shouting out in pain and told him in no uncertain terms, "Shut up, quit acting like a baby, and get back into the game." Only upon closer examination, when he realized that the young player was seriously injured, did the coach begin to show compassion and sensitivity.*

What is it about men that exhibiting emotion seems to be such a terrible thing? What happens to us on the journey of our lives that makes everything good in us seem to die? Why are the eyes that shed tears and the broken hearts terrifying to so many of us? Why is it that the only way to get along as a man is to "keep going, keep moving, and walk it off"? We are fragmented and we begin to split ourselves into mysterious contradictions.

We are sensitive and tenderhearted, mean and competitive, superficial and idealistic. And somehow, somewhere, the young, boy in us who used to dream dreams and see visions is slowly and methodically sacrificed at the altar of manhood. The great Land of Oz where tin men, scarecrows, and cowardly lions can be transformed into the greatest of heroes is slowly transformed into a land where the only thing magical is how much beer a man can drink without throwing up all over himself.

The Masculine Myth

Men are expected to "grow up," which means getting a job and being responsible. Growing up male in Western society means that men have power and need to learn how to exercise control over others. Men are to be recognized as leaders in the home, at work, among friends. Growing up male in Western society means that men have to be strong and tough. It is forbidden for men to express fear, concern, doubt, vulnerability. Men are to be tough-minded and have stamina. Men are also socialized into believing that their bodies must be able to endure untold pain. On the football field, a son who is injured is not to cry; when a girlfriend ends the relationship, boys are taught to move on and not weep. A man's body can never give the impression of weakness, manifested by tears. Crying, after all, is for sissies.

Men are also taught that logic and analysis are the hallmarks of manhood. Emotions might be fine for women, but for men, the key is the ability to think one's way through a situation. Men must be emotionally incompetent—women can take care of the emotional area of life. And finally, men in Western society are driven by their careers, success, and achievement. In fact, careers become the new god for most men. Making it, and making it big is the issue for most men growing up. *How* one makes it big is less important than *if* one makes it big. The following list contains some of the ways the masculine myth is understood:

1. *Life is quantifiable, measurable.*
2. *Anything that can be measured can be controlled. All problems are solvable.*
3. *Questions that cannot be answered should not be asked.*
4. *Knowledge and power are the twin pillars of human identity.*
5. *Anything we can will, we can accomplish.*
6. *Time is chronological, measurable, quantitative (like money), and can be saved or wasted.*
7. *Male conduct should be ruled by the mind.*
8. *Emotion is irrational; sensation, intuition, and feelings are primitive, immature forms of thought.*
9. *The most reasonable, powerful, and controlling individuals are of most value and should govern a society.*
10. *Females are less aggressive, less rational, less valuable than males and, like nature, are to he controlled and excluded from positions of responsibility.*
11. *Child-rearing, homemaking, and the nurturing arts are less important than productive work.*
12. *Money, is the measure of value.*
13. *The chief motivation of men is to accumulate and consume.*
14. *The ultimate goal for men is success as defined by how much wealth one can accumulate.*

Quite a list isn't it? And these descriptors seem to hold true for so many men in our American culture. We have polarized the genders stating rather clearly what behaviors are appropriate for each. Of course, the real problem is that men seem to have no input as to whether the script is true for them. It's as if culture simply dictates and then defines who we are without considering our own unique gifts, talents, and personalities.

On a Journey

Like Dorothy, many of us begin our journeys reluctantly. Suddenly, we are swept up in a cyclone that drops us in a land much like Oz. Everything looks different, smells different, seems different. We discover that the old way of behaving and functioning no longer works in this new land of manhood. What we had learned about the journey, what we thought we knew about this new land is all wrong. We look back at our old homes —our old ways of behaving—and discover that lying beneath the wreckage of our homes is not the Wicked Witch of the East, but rather the old man, with his old thoughts, his old heart, his old fears. Into this world of cowardly lions, tin men, and scarecrows, our God, the Lord Jesus, has put us on a journey of a lifetime. The signposts, a bit fuzzy at first, become clearer as we make our journey toward the Emerald City.

And as we begin our trip down the yellow brick road of manhood, we discover a few rather interesting characters. We discover a Scarecrow who doesn't have a clue what it means to be a man; a Tin Man whose heart is so small that he can't believe it could ever be broken; and a Cowardly Lion who is afraid of many things, most of all, himself. He is afraid to face his own fears and afraid that he might just be a whole lot more than he ever dreamed possible.

The Scarecrow, Tin Man, and Cowardly Lion are, of course, fictional. And this exploration is merely an analogy: not every man will see himself in each—or even one—of these characters. But they serve as handles that guide us through the process as we look at our own psychological, spiritual, and emotional development.

3 *The Scarecrow*

FILLING OUR HEADS WITH MORE THAN STRAW

In the Wizard of Oz, everybody knows what the Scarecrow's problem is: he doesn't have any brains, or at least he thinks he doesn't. That's the problem of scarecrows in general, of course, including many men who have a hard time in relationships. Some men seem to go through life like a breeze. They do well in school. They meet the love of their lives, marry, and live happily ever after. They have children who do well in school and life seems to be one grand adventure after another. They don't worry about too many things because everything seems to come their way. If you asked what they thought about, the usual answer would be, "Not a whole lot." And honestly, they don't. Life just seems to happen for them and happen well.

But there are many men whose heads seem filled with straw. These men have a hard time making it in relationships and life in general. When it comes to growing in relationships with their spouses, their children, their friends, they have a hard time of it. For these men, nothing is a breeze. When their wives ask them to "just open up and share" these men suddenly find themselves lost and confused, unable to think of an adequate reply. It's as if their heads are filled with straw. When family members need love and nurturance, these men can't figure out what to do, let alone what to think about. When asked by anyone, "How do you feel?" the typical answer is either "good" or "bad." That's it.

Scarecrows think—if you can call it thinking—that men must distrust emotions and feelings. At an early age, these men were taught that to show emotional vulnerability is a sign of weakness. When it comes to nurturing, scarecrows have been taught they don't have the stuff. Somehow, our modern culture has taught men to believe that the "stuff" of love is composed of hard work, paying the bills, sex, and maybe a few laughs on the side. And to begin to discuss the importance and prevalence of emotions as if they were really valid and legitimate, well, that's to act and think like a tin man, not a scarecrow. If you want emotions, hearts, nurturance, and tenderness, go seek a heart like a tin man. Scarecrows have better things to do with their time. They have to think great thoughts, solve tremendous problems, analyze, and scrutinize. Scarecrows need brains, not hearts.

What kind of life can a scarecrow have? What kind of relationships can he develop? Where is a scarecrow going to end up? Life is scary business for anybody let alone for men who suspect they have nothing but straw where their brains belong. Life is frightening and depressing for scarecrows because they are never sure of the best course of action.

"Don't talk, don't trust, don't feel" is supposed to be the unwritten law for men. Men are not supposed to talk about things that happen in families, especially if those things deal with the emotional life. We are taught not to trust our emotions or even one another.

Scarecrows have been led to believe that only things you

can see really count. Scarecrows think that things—many things and big things—can make people happy and content. But because their heads are filled with straw, they really don't know what they want. They may be following a track toward career success but are not necessarily excited about the direction the track is leading them in. Often they become slaves to their jobs. In the pursuit of career goals and in the service of providing for their family, they give up creative or artistic endeavors that were important to them in their youth. Dreams have been sacrificed for logical thinking and self-discipline.

These kinds of men—and by the way, I used to be one of them—heads filled with straw, believe that the right way is the masculine way. These men learn throughout their development that they are supposed to adhere to a strict set of unwritten rules about how to handle and express their emotions. They are cautious about any "excessive" emotional expressiveness lest other men construe it as inappropriate. These rules command them to maintain control of themselves at all times; not to let others see how they are feeling; not to be driven by their emotions but by their rational, analytical side; not to feel sad for themselves or someone else, because this is a sign of weakness. For emotional release they play, watch sports, or drink. They show a woman they love her through sex, not by connecting in an intimate, emotionally expressive way.

These ideas regarding emotions and their expression are really the stuff that fills scarecrows' heads. And indeed, the problem is "in the head." Scarecrows see things incorrectly. They become wrong-headed about what really matters in life. And these "straw-filled" ideas are taught to them by their fathers, peer groups, movies, television, and literature. They look to heroes to provide a model, but most of these heroes are distant, emotionless men, deemed strong precisely because they do not let their emotions get in the way. Whether the hero is a basketball player described as the "ice man" because of his calmness in the final seconds of a close game, or a president who doesn't let his fear and compassion block him from committing troops to a war where many young men and women might die, he is admired for his ability to control his emotions. This is not always bad, but it can be extremely limiting.

Shutting Down

As men grow up, they discover that keeping their emotions under control is a formidable task. No matter how hard men try, feelings always emerge in some form or another. Men try to shut down the source of these strong emotional signals to keep themselves from *feeling* anything.

Likewise, men train themselves not to be overly sensitive to the feelings of others since this could evoke their own strong feelings. As boys they learned that empathy is not valued. To be described as "sensitive" or "nice" is considered a put-down, even a dangerous challenge to their manhood. They also learned that nice guys finish last. Not until they were older did they begin to recognize that this axiom is not necessarily true and that they pay a high price for believing it.

The devastating consequences of shutting down their emotional side become evident during a crisis. They are supposed to keep a stiff upper lip in the face of loss. But when men experience grief, whether from the loss of a pet, a friendship, or a family member, they fear that somehow their deep pain is a sign of weakness. They face a startlingly powerful conflict: They are supposed to be strong and silent, yet they feel devastated. They therefore conclude that there must be something terribly wrong with them. They not only feel pain but also feel bad about feeling bad. This supposed weakness must be covered up, disguised, or eliminated. This sense that there is something fundamentally wrong with reacting in certain ways is, I believe, at the core of their feelings of shame.

Many of the men I see who have followed these emotionally restrictive rules for twenty, thirty, or even forty years often appear depressed. They have shut down emotionally. They experience neither intense pain nor intense pleasure. They describe themselves as numb or flat, especially when it comes to relationships. After many years of trying to control or cover up their feelings, scarecrows have succeeded all too well. Yet instead of being proud of their accomplishments, they are like the walking wounded, casualties of a war they were unaware of fighting.

To Care or Be Cared For?

Perhaps the strongest messages scarecrows receive have to do with independence: "be your own man," "don't let anyone push you around," "don't be a mama's boy." These messages are the most confusing. From their earliest years they can remember their fear of being alone. As little children they lived in fear of being separated from their parents. Many men in counseling can recall a common early memory: waiting for Dad to come home from work. It's later than usual for his return. The imagination starts running wild. Something has happened to him. How will the family be able to take care of themselves without their father?

And herein lies the difficulty for every scarecrow who has his head stuffed with the straw of masculine stereotypes: he knows he is supposed to be tough, independent, rugged, yet even as an adult, he is plagued by a desire to be taken care of by someone else.

When scarecrows were young, they looked to their parents for care. Their greatest fear as children was that something would happen to their parents and there would be no one to care for them. They would face the worst situation of all—being abandoned. And as adults, many men transfer that pattern to their wives or girlfriends. This too presents a paradox. As men we learned to be the dominant sex. The message in its most simple form is, "Men are strong, women are weak. A man's job is to protect and take care of the woman in his life." Yet what we are told and what we experience may be two different matters entirely. Our experience tells us we don't always feel so strong and many times the woman in our life appears stronger than we are. Especially when it comes to the emotional realm, we may feel inferior to her.

But this is not easy to accept. A man may see his dependence on his wife as a sign of weakness. After all, he is supposed to be the strong one on whom she can depend. His feelings become confused. Rather than being grateful to his wife for her support, he may tend to downplay the fact, deny it, or worse, get angry with her for her strength. Men's ridicule of women may be a subconscious attempt to regain the upper hand, to reestablish the dominant position they feel is threatened by allowing themselves to need a woman's help. This pattern of moving between emotional dependency on wives and the reassertion of dominance via anger or ridicule becomes a dangerous, destructive dance many men play out in marriage.

This confusion about women and our relationship with them has grown even more profound over the past twenty years of the women's movement. The gender men were taught to view as weak and needy has asserted its strength and independence. Men's expectation of a woman waiting to take care of them when they get home has been dashed. Those women are busy making their way in the world.

It is no longer enough for men to go out and make a living. Now many men need to make a home as well. They need to pitch in at home, doing "women's work," such as washing, cooking, and changing diapers. While some may agree intellectually that it is fair for them to help out with these tasks, they struggle with their ingrained beliefs that these duties are unmanly and unimportant—to be done only to placate an angry wife rather than as meaningful tasks on a par with their work outside the home.

This confusion about relationships with women constitutes a fundamental issue for every man who sees himself as a scarecrow. We will explore this further in chapter nine.

Work, Work, Work

When we ignore our feelings, we make it more difficult to take good care of ourselves. If we spend our entire lives telling ourselves we are serving others—by working too hard, by worrying too much about earning a living, by being engaged in a competitive orientation to life—we usually have little energy left to take care of ourselves. As men overwork, we feel guilty about relaxing with our families, exercising, or just lying in the hammock. Instead, we may eat too much, watch too much TV, or become dependent upon alcohol. Many men also have succumbed to the lure of the sensual—they find themselves involved with pornography or illicit affairs.

"It's Miller time," the beer commercial tells us, showing men hard at work on a manly task, then downing a few after their labors. We know these habits are unhealthy, but they are the only means of relaxation we feel comfortable with or find time for. Consequently, our health deteriorates.

Throughout life the message is to work hard, to be strong and invulnerable. A man imagines himself to be a finely tuned car that is supposed to run without maintenance. "When the going gets tough, the tough get going," we are told and we believe it. The desire to rest or recreate is a weakness unless, of course, you have earned a break by your hard work or good deeds. And although we all know in our guts if not our heads that it's okay to relax, to enjoy, to have fun and play, it doesn't really fit with our masculine image which we have to maintain at all costs. The image is more important than the substance for so many men. We are more concerned about maintaining the facade of having it all together than actually doing whatever is necessary to take care of ourselves and our family. We present an image of kindness, generosity, and love to others outside the family but within our family, everyone else knows better, including ourselves.

What's Wrong?

We are hurt, emotionally, relationally, spiritually, but because we don't allow ourselves to be aware of the extent of our wounds, we can't take steps toward healing and health. Our problem as scarecrows is not stupidity, but a lack of objectivity.

Because of this, we fail to see the reality of pain, hurt, and anger in our lives.

Do you know any of these men?

- *A college student was considered "the life of the party." He was intelligent, witty, and sociable, but when he was alone, he experienced deep loneliness and resentment.*
- *A businessman who, as a child, was neglected by his ambitious father, thought, "If I can just get that promotion, then I'll be happy. Success is what really counts in life!" He got many promotions and raises because he was driven to perform well, but happiness continued to elude him.*
- *A husband with three children spends long hours at the office and wonders, "Why don't I feel close to my wife?" Having grown up with an alcoholic father and a demanding mother, this man has never felt lovable, and so isn't able to receive his wife's love.*
- *An articulate pastor speaks powerfully about the unconditional love and grace of God, yet he is plagued by guilt. He is driven to succeed in his public ministry, but is passive and withdrawn around his family. He has never understood how to apply his own teaching to his life and relationships.*

We all have experienced the inability to think clearly about our experiences, thoughts, and behaviors in different circumstances. We all have sensed that maybe our heads are filled with straw after all because so much of what we have been taught seems wrong. I began to realize that many of the ideas regarding manhood that I had been taught growing up were straw when I entered the counseling profession. Before that time, whenever I felt the pain of rejection, the sting of sarcasm, or anything less than the complete approval of others, I tried to shrug it off. I reasoned that because of my status as a Christian and as a pastor, I should convey an attitude of happiness and contentment in all things. When something didn't go the way I'd hoped or planned, I simply told myself it didn't really matter. Though I was able to fool myself in these instances, my gloomy countenance told those who were closest to me another story:

A good friend inquired about what was wrong. "You seem troubled," he said. "Is anything bothering you?"

"Me? No, I'm fine."

"You don't seem fine to me," he persisted. "You're acting as though you might be depressed about something."

I stuck to my time-tested text. "No, really, I am fine. I guess I've just been a little pressured lately." The truth was that I did have some very personal issues that I wanted resolved with my father. I had to talk to him about something that concerned me and my family greatly but I was incredibly afraid to even broach the issue. I kept it bottled up and went right along as if everything was okay.

Several weeks later, my friend again inquired about my well-being. This time, I was brave enough to admit that something was going on. I briefly told him about the issue with my dad and said, "Realizing how hurt and afraid I was to speak to my father has also enabled me to be honest with the Lord about my feelings and begin working through them."

"I'm sorry about what happened," he said, "but I appreciate your honesty, and think it's great that you're doing something constructive with a difficult situation."

Over time, I began to confide in this friend about other problems I encountered. He helped me a great deal. At times he would say, "Here's how I'd feel in your situation. I'd be angry because ... Do you feel angry?" Or "I'd be hurt because ... Do you feel hurt?"

In the light of this honesty and love, and through the gracious work of the Holy Spirit, I began to be honest with myself and with God. The tough exterior I had developed started cracking, and I began to experience the pain I had neither wanted nor allowed myself to feel. This was hardly pleasant, but acknowledging the presence of hurt in my life was my first step toward comfort.

What's Missing?

Why do so many men lack the ability to think clearly about what really matters in life? Why can't we see the reality of our lives? Why are so we so afraid to open the windows, turn on the lights, and allow the light in our lives?

We have been socialized into keeping our heads filled with straw. We think our masculine situations are normal and experiencing loneliness, hurt, anger, and fear is part and parcel of what it means to grow up male. Perhaps we also want to be "good Christians," and believing that good Christian men don't have problems or feelings like ours, we deny the existence of our painful emotions. Many men have learned from childhood that if they act a particular way they may lose the love they so desperately need. So men discover rather early on that to be loved, nurtured, and accepted means that a very real part of their personality has to be denied.

We develop elaborate defense mechanisms to block the pain in our lives. We suppress emotions; we are compulsive perfectionists; we drive ourselves to succeed or we withdraw and become passive; we attack people who hurt us; we punish ourselves when we fail; we try to say clever things to be accepted; we help people so we will be appreciated; and we say and do countless other things.

But we realize something is missing—there has to be more to life than this. Even the Scarecrow in *The Wizard of Oz*, whose head was filled with straw, knew that there had to be more. He knew he could have a brain; he knew someone could give it to him. And so it is with all scarecrows. Some of us may not be cowardly lions and thus have the courage to examine ourselves. We may desperately want to change, but are unsure how and where to start. We may refuse to look honestly within for fear of what we'll find, or we may be afraid that even if we can discover what's wrong, nothing can help us. "This is the way I am. I was this way in the beginning, am now and ever shall be, world without end," we tell ourselves.

It is difficult to deal with these issues in a forthright manner. We hide from ourselves. We cover up. We hide from others too. We act as if scarecrows are all we were ever meant to be. We are afraid to step out and maybe look at ourselves objectively and examine where we might possibly change. Like the Scarecrow who needed help from Dorothy to climb down from the wooden post which held him as a scarecrow, we too need help to climb down from the "masculine heights" to the real world where we can be really touched. Of course, this is much more than just needing help psychologically. We need God's help spiritually as well. We all need to be changed. We all need to be made new. We all need new ways to think because we also need new hearts and new wills. We are desperately in need of a makeover, men and women alike. The Bible says we were born "dead in our transgressions and sins" (Ephesians 2:1). Scarecrows, tin men, and cowardly lions—all of us—can't be made alive unless He who made the heavens and the earth, He who was hung on the wooden pole of Calvary comes down to make us alive. Dead scarecrows can't think; dead tin men can't feel; and dead cowardly lions don't have courage. They are all very dead of very dead. And the most powerful force of all is our great Shepherd of the sheep, scarecrows, tin men, and cowardly lions, who has come to bring us life. We all are in need of being made alive—given real life. Jesus Christ, in His grand and glorious life, death, and resurrection has won us to

Himself and made us all new. The only way for me to begin to think clearly about myself as a man is to begin to think clearly about Him who is the God-man, Jesus Christ, the Lord.

Because He has made us alive, with His strength and grace through the power of the Holy Spirit, I can begin to look at my life as a man, as a husband, as a father. This, however, is not an easy thing to do. Some of us have deep emotional and spiritual scars resulting from neglect, abuse, and manipulation that often accompany living in a dysfunctional family (alcoholism, drug abuse, divorce, absent father or mother, excessive anger, verbal and/or physical abuse, etc.), but all of us bear the effects of our own sinful nature and the imperfections of others.

Whether your hurts are deep or relatively mild, it is wise to be honest about them in the context of affirming relationships so healing can begin.

Honesty

Many men mistakenly believe that God doesn't want us to be honest about our lives. We think He will be upset with us if we tell Him how we really feel. But the Scriptures tell us that God does not want us to be superficial—in our relationship with Him, with others, or in our own lives. David wrote, "Surely you desire truth in the inner parts; you teach me wisdom in the inmost place" (Psalm 51:6).

The Lord desires truth and honesty at the deepest level, and wants us to experience His love, forgiveness, and power in all areas of our lives. Experiencing His love does not mean that all of our thoughts, emotions, and behaviors will be pleasant and pure. It means that we can be real, feeling pain and joy, love and anger, confidence and confusion.

Even though we have heads filled with straw, scarecrows —every last one of us—have been redeemed, bought back by the death and resurrection of Jesus Christ. We have been made new and it is now possible to begin to think differently about ourselves, others, our world, our God, and our lives. We have been created for more than simply hanging around and frittering away our time in this world. We have been destined for greatness because we have a great God who has done great things for us.

To See or Not to See

With brand-new brains, new ways of thinking, former scarecrows can be very much aware of the dictum of Socrates that "the unexamined life is not worth living." Men can be thoughtful and reflective. Men are capable of asking the right questions of life and relationships, and flexible enough to let life question them. Instead of simply believing "that's the way men are," men who have been made new by the Gospel of Christ refuse to live an unreflected life in an unexamined world. They want to set their hearts, minds, and wills on things that matter—the stuff of life that really counts, that really makes a difference. They understand that what really matters is not what you can see but what you can't see. Too many men go along believing that the things we can see are real—the homes, the boats, the money, the careers, the toys. We spend our entire lives and sometimes ourselves trying to accumulate things. But the things you can't see—love, hope, forgiveness—are so much more real than anything you can see. Questions such as "Where am I with you?" and "Where are you with me?" are the questions of significance. And frankly, in the difficult moments of our lives, we all realize this is true.

A tragic story will illustrate the point:

A couple was ready for a long-awaited trip to Florida. They had worked for months to plan and prepare for this trip and were excited about the opportunity to get away with each other and their two kids, a 10-year-old girl and 5-year-old boy. They made their way to Florida and, as their car crossed the Florida-Georgia line, the father saw in the distance ahead headlights coming straight for them. He tried to steer to the side of the road but before he was able to move over far enough, the other car hit them head-on going 60 miles per hour. His wife was killed upon impact. His young daughter was killed immediately. His young son was critically injured. But for some reason, because of his position in the car or the airbag's effectiveness, he survived the crash relatively uninjured.

The father made the trip back to St. Louis where his beloved wife and daughter were laid to rest. Immediately after the funeral service was concluded, he got on a plane to be with his son who was in a coma in a Florida hospital. As the father entered the hospital, he was greeted by the doctors who informed him that his 5-year-old son was brain dead and they needed his permission to stop all life support. The father was devastated. He had just buried his wife and daughter and now was met with this horrible news. He stood there, stunned. He gave the doctors permission to stop life support but asked for ten minutes with his boy first. He wanted to say good-bye.

I wasn't with the father at the time of his good-bye to his son, but I can tell you this: He didn't talk about things you can see. He didn't pull out his wallet and talk to his son about his major credit cards. He didn't take out pictures of their nice home in the suburbs and talk about how big it was. He didn't describe in detail their flashy sports cars. He didn't talk about his son's grades and how good they were and how he had the best clothes in his school. He didn't talk about any of the things that we seem to think are so very important in our world. Rather he talked about things you can't see. He talked about his love for his son and how he was the apple of his eye. He talked about how he would soon see his mother and sister and how they were waiting for him in heaven. But most important, he talked about Jesus. He talked about how Jesus had loved the son so much that He came to earth and became a child, and then He suffered and died and rose again so everyone could be saved. He talked about the forgiveness of sins Jesus had won for all people and because his little boy had been baptized and knew Jesus as his Savior, he too would be in heaven.

You see, you put people in the trenches of life and what they think is real changes drastically. The only things that matter are "Where are we?" and "Where is God?" and "Do you know how very much I love you?" And yet something in our lives seems to get in the way of our expression of those realities. We become "junktified." Our minds become cluttered. We focus on things that, in the greater scheme, don't matter. And in the meantime, the people who do matter are somehow pushed aside.

Simply living my life for these past 47 years has convinced me that the only thing of value we can give others is what we are, not what we have. Too many people give external things. But in the trenches, we learn that those aren't the most important things. Whether it is with our spouse or our children, our extended family or our friends and acquaintances, the most essential thing we have to give is who and what we are.

A New Man

God calls us to live a full life—not a narrowed life or constricted life—a full life. Men are called to use all their capacities—their hearts, their wills, their minds. A deep, personal peace is the promise and legacy of Jesus to His followers. When our lives become narrowed, or conflicted, or our peace is interrupted by discomfort, whether physical, emotional, or behavioral, the experience is an invitation to think differently. It is an invitation for personal reflection. "What is in me?" is the necessary and sometimes painful question that must be asked. I cannot change others, the world about me, the weather, or the position of the stars. I can, however, change myself. In reflection and prayer, in study of God's Word, and mutual conversation with trusted confidants, I can trace my discomfort to an unhealthy way of thinking. I have been duped into believing that my head is filled with straw. I can look clearly at what is in me. And this is the area of my thoughts and attitudes that I can control and change. There may be times when my attitude is found to be in full harmony with my Christian faith. But most of the time, if you are like me, you will find a neurotic and un-Christian attitude at the source of many problems facing all people, particularly men.

And because of the new life and mind that Christ has given me, I now have the ability to ask myself about different ways of thinking, seeing, and believing. I can reach out to others in my need, to explore with the thoughts and mind and attitudes of another who does not seem to be afflicted with my discomfort. I can discover what right thinking really is. And as I go out and explore with my mind the new insights and ways of viewing the world around me, I discover that the brain I've been searching for has been there all along. I am redeemed by Christ —He already implanted within me a new mind for seeing life the way it really is meant to be seen. With all its grandeur and wonder, life is a gift from God to be lived, to be used, to be engaged in, to be enjoyed.

> *A man was walking the beach and picked up an old, dried-out starfish. With great care he put it back in the water. He said, "It's just dried out but when it gets moisture again, it's going to come back to life." And then he thought for a moment and said, "You know, maybe that's the whole process of becoming, maybe we get to the point where we sort of dry out, and all we need is a little moisture to get us started again."*

The waters of Holy Baptism came to my dried up, sin-filled life and gave me new life. Through the sparkling waters of Holy Baptism, the Holy Spirit cleansed me, forgave me, and set me on a new path. Or as St. Paul said to Titus, "He saved us, not because of righteous things we had done, but because of His mercy. He saved us through the washing of rebirth and renewal by the Holy Spirit, whom He poured out on us generously through Jesus Christ our Savior, so that, having been justified by His grace, we might become heirs having the hope of eternal life" (Titus 3:5-7).

I am alive! It needn't have been so. And what is it like to be alive in perhaps the only place where life is? We have been given the opportunity to live a day of it and see. We can take any day and be alive in it. No one claims that it will be entirely painless, but no matter. It is your day and the world is open to you to explore with all the great thoughts you can muster. Have fun, delight in yourself, delight in the God who gave you Himself; delight in the world and in those around you.

4 The Tin Man

GOD, GIVE ME A HEART!

The Tin Man in *The Wizard of Oz* was convinced he didn't have a heart. He was convinced he was some kind of freak, lacking some basic quality to his life. There are many tin men in our world today. They somehow feel differently than other human beings feel. Some of the things that make other people laugh make these men want to cry, and sometimes the other way around. These men don't make friends as easily as they wish they did, and there are times when they almost feel like a creature from another planet. Tin men long for home, but they are not sure where home is. Tin men hunger for relationships, but they aren't sure they will ever have any that matter.

If you're a tin man, you can be lonely even when you're surrounded by people you've known all your life. You wonder if anybody is ever going to love you the way you read about in books. You wonder if you're ever going to find anybody you can love that way yourself.

More than anything else in the world, tin men want a heart they can call home—a place where they are safe and secure and loved, and a person with whom they can share their innermost self. But they also believe, like the tin man in the movie, that they will never find it. They have their hopes. They start down the yellow brick road to Oz, hoping against hope that maybe someone can help them in their quest. But for all practical purposes, these men have rusted shut to the world, to themselves, and to others. Because loving and being loved can be so very painful, these men have hardened themselves against feelings and closeness. Oh, maybe a long time ago these men were filled with great hearts, but the greater one's heart, the greater the possibility of pain—and for these tin men, the pain is unbearable. As a result, these men become invulnerable. Their armor becomes their refusal to feel—to feel pain, sadness, hurt. And as time marches on, tin men begin to hold people at a distance. They have a hard time connecting. They try to carry on conversations about sports, the weather, maybe politics, but anything remotely dealing with the heart is off-limits. As a result of this distancing, tin men begin to wonder what's wrong. They begin to believe that maybe they don't have hearts. Pound on their chests and all you hear are loud, empty echoes.

An Internal Struggle

Tin men's wish not to feel, to get those stupid feelings out of their heads and hearts is typical of how we men have been raised to regard feelings. Rather than viewing feelings as a natural, biologically based reaction to events in our lives, we have been taught to view them as a nuisance, an inconvenience, an unwelcome interloper. It is not that we are taught that feelings do not exist, but rather that being a man requires us to keep our feelings under control. It is as if we harbor an internal competition between the good guys—the mind, self-discipline, rationality—and the bad guys—feelings, impulses, emotionality. The outcome of this battle determines our status as men. The judges include our parents and our peers but most of all, ourselves.

This unhealthy internal struggle can confound us throughout our lives. As young men, we struggle to learn the rules of the game. But when we later move into committed relationships, we begin to hear conflicting messages, especially from our wives who urge us to be more expressive of our feelings. "Why can't you be more in touch with your feelings?" "Why don't you ever tell me how you feel?" "Strong men aren't afraid of their feelings."

In the workplace, however, the same old messages are reinforced: "Don't let your feelings get in the way of being an effective leader." "Don't be overly emotional with your clients." "Just do your job and don't ask questions." "What we're after is results, not your feelings."

And what do we want ourselves? We're often not sure. After years of trying to keep our feelings at bay, by midlife we may be left clueless about our true wants and needs. We rarely trust the emotional cues available to us. Instead, we follow the blueprint society provides to determine what we need and want —a good job, possessions, prestige, and power, all earned through hard work and preferably without complaints.

The Crushed Spirit

One of the greatest crimes of humanity is to destroy the spirit of a child. There seems to be a natural sense of wonder and awe in the lives of children. Yet this wonder, mystery and magic easily can be crushed out of a child. And if the boyhood spirit is lost, the man can spend his life trying to find it. If the boyhood spirit is wounded, the man can spend a lifetime trying to recover. It may be hard to recover from physical harm, from loss of security, or income, or family members, but recovering from a broken spirit is the hardest of all.

Tin men have had their hearts destroyed. Call it heart, spirit, soul, or spark, it is what makes us distinctively us, human. It is a combination of self-esteem, a positive mental attitude, a belief in yourself, and a strong sense of identity that cannot easily be defeated. People who have hearts are those who want to live life fully. They want to engage people and the world around them. Men with hearts use all of their human faculties, powers, and talents. They are comfortable with and open to the full experience and expression of all human emotions. Men with hearts are vibrantly alive in mind, heart, and will.

An Alive Heart

There is an instinctive fear in most of us, I think, to travel with our engines at full throttle. We prefer, for the sake of safety, to take life in small and dainty doses. Men with hearts travel with confidence that if one is *alive* in every aspect of his life, the result will be harmony, not chaos.

When you have a heart, you are fully engaged in what you are doing. You hold nothing back. Without a heart, you go through the motions of your life. With a heart, you are life.

Remember what it was like growing up as a boy? Remember playing games and giving it all you had? If you dove for a pass in football, you hung in the air and stretched to the limit, reaching for all you were worth. You ran like the wind and never quit until your body finally quit for you. Every relationship and friendship was passionate. Everything seemed to count. Indeed, St. Paul's words ring loudly and clearly for young boys growing up, "Whatever you do, do it all for the glory of God" (1 Corinthians 10:31). Whether it was for the glory of God could certainly be debated. But whatever it was we did when we were growing up, we did it with all our strength (oftentimes, for our own glory because of our sinfulness, but we did it with passion).

We know the heart exists—not simply the organic muscle that beats in our chests, but the heart that makes us wonderfully unique and alive—the spirit, that part of us that can take an ordinary moment and transform it into something wonderful and beautiful. But this special part of us has largely been ignored by many researchers studying why some people endure hardship and remain healthy. We've all known boys who were raised under very difficult circumstances yet were always upbeat and grew up to be healthy men. What was different about these boys compared to those who emerged from dysfunctional families only to carry on the dysfunction? I have had students in many of my classes who give clear evidence of somehow having lost their heart, their spirit, their passion for life. Nothing seems to motivate them. Nothing seems to inspire them. There is nothing in their lives, no higher goal or aspiration that moves them to great passion. They seem, as it were, the "living dead."

When men try to recover from a painful childhood, it is not long-term therapy or the analysis of victimization that allows them to heal. Rather it is finding their hearts. There can be no growth or recovery, no liveliness, without somehow finding the heart.

A Childlike Heart

For so many men today, the problem is not going back to find their "inner child," but rather discovering their hearts that beat with passion for life, for people, for relationships. When I discuss these concepts at workshops and conferences, I often get puzzled looks. Men who attend the conferences seldom seem to understand what I'm driving at. They look confused and it seems that I'm talking to the wind. So I offer an example from my own life that might be helpful.

> *When I was 17 years old, I was dating the girl of my dreams. It was the fall of my senior year in high school and Mary Lopez was the absolute love of my life. We had spent the whole day together with her family and finally returned home for dinner and some relaxing moments in Mary's living room. It was just me, Mary, and the soft music of the stereo. I don't remember where her two brothers and sister were, or if her parents were in the kitchen listening to our conversation. What I do remember was sitting next to Mary as her hand reached out to gently clasp my hand in hers.*
>
> *I remember that moment vividly. Everything around me seemed to drop away. A strange stillness drowned out the noise of the stereo. The music of Styx's big hit, "Come Sail Away," playing in the background was silenced by the magic of the moment. Between the delightful smells of Mary's shampoo and her perfume, I was intoxicated. Her*

touch held not only my hand but also my heart. For me, that moment belonged to another dimension of time and space. And I took it in—that incredible moment, that delicate touch of her hand on mine.

I was awestruck! Full of wonder! And I remember saying these simple words to myself as I walked home later that evening: "Bryan! She loves you! She loves you! She loves you!"

Call it what you will—puppy love, infatuation, silly romance. But whatever it was, for those few moments, I was incredibly alive. It was with a heightened awareness, a hyper-intensive consciousness, that I held that moment far too wonderful to describe. In a mystical way, I stepped out of myself at that moment and reflected upon myself experiencing it.

I do not know how long I will live, but if I were to live a million years, I would remember that moment because I truly lived it.

An Awakening of the Heart

During those moments it's as if the whole universe has come into being. There is a brilliance to our lives and it almost seems as if we are awakening from a deep, dark sleep. As Victor Hugo said when he went out at twilight to gaze upon the city:

For a long time, I remained motionless, letting myself be penetrated gently by this unspeakable ensemble, by the serenity of the sky and the melancholy of the moment. I do not know what was going on in my mind, and I could not express it; it was one of those ineffable moments when one feels something in himself which is going to sleep and something which is awakening.[4]

Life is suddenly awakened and we know we are living. I'm afraid that many tin men are on a merry-go-round of accomplishments or crises, trying to find the meaning in their lives that escaped when their spirit died an early death. Although awake, they seem to be quite asleep. I'm afraid that somehow the "ordinariness of life" has led to a dullness toward living where nothing really matters anymore. I'm speaking as a tin man to other tin men, of course, but have you ever thought that if you don't feel good about yourself today, what is bothering you is not your job, your relationships, or the mortgage, but lack of heart for anything that matters? Childhood may be over, but childhood wounds can still be felt in adulthood. Maybe the real problem is not that these wounds didn't end when childhood was over, but that they ended childhood for you. You and your wounds were forced to adjust, and part of the adjustment was to give up being a child. And as a result you lost the sense of childlike wonder that accompanies growing up.

Recently, I heard about a world-famous musician who is deaf. She plays on stages around the world, and many orchestras want to accompany her because she is so talented. During an interview, she commented that when the doctor told her at age eight she was deaf due to an injury and her musical career was over, everyone was visibly upset. She replied, "You don't think that a little comment like that, saying I was deaf, was going to affect my musical career, do you?" It didn't, and today she is one of the world's best musicians.

She related that this tragic time proved to be a blessing in disguise. She claims that she saw and "heard" things entirely differently for the first time. She maintains that society had trained her to take the world for granted. But the hold society had on her has been broken by her deafness.

The world proved miraculously new and strangely wonderful to her. Along with her renewed passion to play music, she put to use her creative imagination. Her reengagement with the world was accomplished by a sense of awe and a new passion for discovery that others seldom know. She claims her excitement for life was intensified beyond anything that would have been possible had she been able to hear.

Tin men who long for hearts long for these kinds of experiences. They need a liveliness and an awareness that the musician experienced. It is about engaging the world as I momentarily did when I sat holding hands with Mary. It is an attempted exploration into the kind of heightened experience that goes beyond happiness and is hinted at in the biblical promise of joy.

Can You Have a New Heart?

Of course, more than anything else, tin men need to know that they need new hearts and they can have them. The prophet Jeremiah said, "The heart is deceitful above all things and beyond cure. Who can understand it?" (Jeremiah 17:9). The heart is indeed that—wicked from the time of birth. Paul said we were "dead in [our] transgressions and sins" (Ephesians 2:1).

The startling fact of Scripture is that every man—and every woman for that matter—needs a new heart because the old one is dead. Spiritually, all of us were lost, blind, dead, and enemies of God. Spiritually, our hearts were broken because of our own sinfulness.

Adam had a heart pure and holy. His heart beat with a passion for God, for himself, and the world around him. God said repeatedly, "This is good." Man's heart was good, created in the image of God Himself. All was holy and right and decent. But then Adam's heart was broken and, along with it, the rest of the world's as well, including our Lord's. In all of creation, no creature compared to Adam. Indeed, Adam was a magnificent creation, complete and perfect in the image of God, designed to reign over all the earth. Through man, God wanted to demonstrate His holiness (Psalm 99:3-5); love and patience (1 Corinthians 13:4); forbearance (1 Corinthians 13:7); wisdom (James 3:13, 77); comfort (2 Corinthians 1:3-4); forgiveness (Hebrews 10:17); faithfulness (Psalm 89:1-2, 5, 8); and grace (Psalm 111:4). Through his intellect, his will, and his heart, man was to be the showcase for God's glorious character.

But then Adam chose to forsake his heart's one desire, his God, and follow Eve into sin. Adam thus lost the image and the heart of God. The man who once walked with God in the glorious garden is now ashamed to be with God. And when questioned, "Where are you?" his now wicked heart turns on the very one he had been given to love—his wife. "Yes," the man admits, he did eat the forbidden fruit, but only because he was tempted by "the woman whom You gave me." And since that day, every man, woman, and child has also been born in need of a new heart—a heart that can beat for something other than self.

The cross of Jesus Christ challenges the notion that our hearts are pure and holy. The cross challenges any idea that we are basically nice people who are making progress, that all we need is better education, better economic systems, better effort, and we shall be good. Jesus Christ was crucified by everything people hold dear—religious ideals, governmental orders, democracy in action, social revolution, biblical religion, tradition, national self-determination. They were all there at the foot of the cross as He bled and died.

So the story of Jesus reveals who we are even as it reveals who God is. We live in a fallen world that treats its Savior and its criminals in the same way, where the criminals are as likely to be those who wear black robes and sit in judgment as those upon whom we pass the sentence of death. The cross is God's *no* to humanity's aspiration and delusions.

Yet the cross is also God's *yes* to humanity as God takes unto Himself humanity's sins and rejection. God beats into us new hearts! Our awareness of our sin comes after hearing the story of Jesus, not before. We can only know the depth and seriousness of our sin when viewed through the perspective of the selfless love of Christ. Our sin is so serious, so deep-rooted in our thoughts and actions, that we are as incapable of seeing it as a fish is incapable of noticing water.

This is incredibly important for men who desire new hearts. They first need to know that their old ones are wrong. But not simply wrong, because the word implies that the problem can be corrected. Our hearts are *dead* wrong. They are very dead of very dead. Oh, we say that often we act out of love —our "love" is but calculating egotism, an attempt to somehow subsume the interests of others into those of the self. We call sin "mistakes" or "ignorance," or justify it by the circumstances of our social background, economic condition, or some other factor that gets the blame off our back. Our confessions of sin are thus so much play-acting, posturing, and other perverted attempts to look out for ourselves.

The story of Jesus' heart helps us to be honest about our own heart stories, not to hide from or despise our humanity because God did not deem it an unworthy thing to become human. We need not lie about ourselves because the scriptural story is of a Savior, who, even as He is hanging on a cross, says, "Father, forgive." Indeed, God's very nature is revealed as One who eats and drinks with sinners, who comes to seek and to save the lost. We need not hide from the gaze of this God. Nor must we hide our sinfulness from ourselves and others.

What to Do with This New Heart?

Tin men with new hearts are enabled through Christ finally to look at themselves for who they really are. I have not been all that I say I have been. I am not quite what I want to be. I have hurt those who love me rather than love them in response. I have not been the kind of man my wife, my kids, and my friends need. Yet now, in Christ, I am also much more than I ever dreamed possible. I am sinner *and* saint! I am forgiven, redeemed. I have been loved into life by the very living Son of God who loved me and gave Himself for me. I am now good and at times bad. Because of the Lord Jesus, I can at last be honest about who I am with those who love me. Real tragedy does happen in my life. Things have not always turned out the way I wanted them to. But the story of Jesus tells us that God is willing even to enter into my real tragedy, my real story my real life, to give me a new heart that beats for Him.

The Real Story

So the story of my being a Christian, someone who answers to a crucified God, enables me to claim the story of being a man as my own. Because I am forgiven, I am able to see and to admit my story just as it is. The fear of God is the beginning of wisdom.

The great church father, St. Augustine, says in his confessions that our life story seems like a chicken yard full of patternless tracks until, in the light of Jesus' redemption of us, we come to see that this meaningless maze, this mess, has actually been a story of constant forgiveness and persistent grace. We look back on our lives and see the hand of God tugging at our hearts until we were able to turn to God in love and thanksgiving. Our lives—even their worst, darkest, and most evil parts—are transformed into the means of our deliverance.

To encounter this story of Jesus is to be freed from the false stories that grip so many of our lives—stories of "real men," "macho males," "stereotypical masculinity," the "masculine ideal." This story enables us to live without props or protection other than the truthfulness and love of God. And what a good story it is. Only a story this interesting—so cosmic, so daring, so real—could have the power to overcome our fatal self-absorption by directing our gaze to how marvelously the Lord of the universe is reaching out to us through the cross and resurrection of Jesus.

When all is said and done, my life has significance and interest to you only as an example of how even the tragedies and revelations in my life have been used by God to lead me to the Truth, which is Jesus Christ.

Having said all this, however, I want to caution you against taking too pessimistic a reading of our human condition. Too many Christians believe and teach that because we are sinful from birth, nothing good can come from us in this life. Many Christians also strongly imply that life lived in this world is simply a vale of tears where there is no happiness or joy. We simply wait for the sweet "bye and bye." But the story of Jesus challenges this pessimistic world-view. For one thing, the humans we sometimes despise are also the people among whom our Savior chose to make His home. For another, Jesus Christ is Lord. "In the world you have tribulation," He says. Then, perhaps with a twinkle in His eye, He adds, "But take heart! I have overcome the world" (John 16:33).

God has won! Jesus is Lord. By His glorious death and resurrection, sin, death, Satan, and hell are defeated. The triumph of the grace of God in Christ is the melody underlying the various subplots and movements of the story of Jesus. The Christian knows something the world does not: "God was reconciling the world to Himself in Christ" (2 Corinthians 5:19).

Salvation is already accomplished. We cannot add to it. All we can do as men of God is proclaim that it has happened. We have new hearts after all! We can love. We can confront the demons that terrify us and send them scurrying with the words, "Christ is Victor!" We can adjust our lives in accordance with the love story. We can gather together to proclaim the victory that is ours in Christ, to tell the story and to celebrate our deliverance.

Tin men—on their way to the Emerald City—already

have new hearts and now want to help others, maybe a few scarecrows, cowardly lions, or even a few more tin men make the journey as well. Tin men have astoundingly optimistic faith based upon the conviction, which is itself based upon the Easter story that Jesus is Victor. Here is God in human form, and no earthly or demonic power can withstand or defy the living God. Here is a holy optimism that does not deny the problems all men face, yet which testifies that every problem, evil, and sin has been defeated through the victory of Christ.

When all is said and done regarding men and their issues, when every psychological assessment has been taken and men have been analyzed, scrutinized, and categorized, we still have to account for the work of Christ on the cross. Was God in Christ reconciling the world to Himself, making a full, perfect, and sufficient sacrifice for the sins of the whole world? Before we can confront the many psychological problems facing men, we must stand as people confident of the great work of Christ on the cross. We are men, but men made new.

The story of our Lord Jesus still unfolds, in your life and mine. Sin and evil may be defeated, but they lurk in our lives. This heart that beats for the Lord still, somehow, someway beats for sin, and self, and self-centeredness. So, in Christ, we continue to live out the story of His combat with the forces of darkness, "For He must reign until He has put all His enemies under His feet. The last enemy to be destroyed is death" (1 Corinthians 15:25-26).

I have found incredible strength in knowing that because I am loved—loved by my God in Christ who knows me, warts and all—I can begin the process of knowing myself as well. The inward journey is difficult for so many men because they fear what they will find on the journey. We have hidden too many things from ourselves and our awareness. We don't like what we are. We want to be more. But we must do our best to take a full, sober look at who we really are. We shall have no real humanness until we understand why we rely upon stereotypical images, roles, and others to define who we are.

Self-examination at its best, whether conducted through the tools of theology, psychology, or literature, is an investigation of how we adopted the lie for our standard of living. The lie which is culture itself, the lie which promises that if certain manly behaviors are followed then eventually you will be rewarded with your heart's desires. But this lie, in the end, always fails to deliver. What is the lie we are living? How high are the costs of living this lie? Is there any way to be honest and still live as a man?

Although many of us might struggle with the answers to these questions, we are prepared for the struggle. We are equipped to deal with these questions that gnaw at us and plague us all our lives. We can consider how it is that our hearts still beat fervently with passion for God, the world, others, ourselves, and life. We can fully engage this world, not because we or the world are so good, but because God is good and He has entered this world and our lives in the person of His Son, Jesus Christ.

Our ultimate problem, of course, is not masculinity, though it may be part of the issue. Our ultimate problem is mortality. All other issues are simply manifestations of that ultimate problem. Try as we may, our heroic attempts to overcome this problem always end in failure.

But the Bible presents another story another life, another

tale of a different heart—the heart of God broken by our sin, but resurrected and beating in the life of God's Son, Jesus Christ. This is our destiny—not oblivion, but communion. Through the ages, Christianity says, we have strained forward, constantly reaching out to the eternal, yet always finding it beyond our reach. So, to our surprise, on a cold night in Bethlehem, the Eternal reached out to us, became one of us so we might become one with the Eternal. Through the ages, we built our grand illusions out across the chasm of great, dark, unmentionable death, never succeeding in bridging the gulf to the infinite. So, on a Friday noon, outside Jerusalem, a cross was raised and Infinite Love climbed up on it, embraced death, triumphed, and showed us the way to freedom.

This is the surprising story that makes honesty possible. This is the story to end all stories, where the Savior stoops and gives every last one of us our desire—new hearts and lives for old ones.

5 *The Cowardly Lion*

GOD, GIVE ME STRENGTH TO STAND MY GROUND

All of us know what the problem was for the Cowardly Lion in *The Wizard of Oz*—he was a coward. He was afraid to act. He thought about the great world out there with all its wonders and didn't worry so much that he didn't have brains enough to handle it as that he didn't have guts enough to survive in it. Upon meeting the Cowardly Lion, all the Oz characters—Dorothy, the Tin Man, the Scarecrow and even the little dog, Toto—were terrified. He presented such a petrifying image. As the characters skipped through the road chanting, "Lions and tigers and bears, oh my!" the Lion pounced on them from the woods. He let out an enormous growl, terrifying everyone. But to everyone's surprise, the brave Lion became a sniveling coward when Dorothy, in anger, slapped him on the nose. Beneath the mask, he was frightened—even of his own shadow.

Many men are just like the Cowardly Lion. On the outside we present an image of strength and toughness. We bellow, we growl, and make all the manly noises we can think of. We give the impression that of all the things we may be, we are not cowards. But as it was with the Cowardly Lion, so it is with us

—our bark, or rather growl, is worse than our bite.

Many men find themselves in the very same situation as the Cowardly Lion. All they can do is say how brave and courageous they are when, in reality, just the opposite is true. We are afraid of so many things. We fear commitment. We fear our emotions. We fear intimacy. We fear we won't measure up to the image our loved ones have of us. We fear, for one reason or another, that if we we're really found out, our world would crumble around us. But most important, we are afraid to stay put—to stay where we are once we have given our word that we will stay. Commitment and fidelity to family, wife, and kids scare many men. They look around at those who have gone before them and wonder, "How in the world did they do it?" They watch couples who have kept their vows of faithfulness for fifty years and wonder how it is possible. They raised children. They acquired homes and cars and refrigerators, and kept them more or less in repair. They held down jobs and paid their taxes. Generally speaking, these men who have gone before us seemed to be in charge of their lives, independent, resourceful, and able to cope with reality in ways we couldn't believe ourselves capable of even if we had a hundred years to work on it. We need courage.

So what does it mean to be a courageous man? How does courage manifest itself in you and me as we make our way? One of the best ways to get at this issue is to ask these questions: What has become of a life lived well? What has happened to a noble life—a life lived according to the divine plan of God? What has happened to the idea that men are always men of their words and their word is their bond? What has happened that today what most typifies many men is the inability or the unwillingness to "stay put"? Too many men are leaving their commitments. Too many are turning back on their word. Too many men make decisions based solely on how they happen to feel at the moment.

I would suggest that now, more than any other time in our history we need men of courage. The statistics are staggering: men are leaving their families, their wives, their children, and their homes like never before. And this is just as prevalent within "Christian homes" as in non-Christian homes. In the name of "finding oneself" and clichés such as "God wouldn't want me to be unhappy," men are abandoning their commitments at alarming rates. They are, in effect, cowards.

What about Responsibility?

In any age, courage is the simple virtue needed for a human being to walk the rocky road from infancy to adulthood. But in an age like ours, where morality is defined by one's own personal whims, desires, and pleasures, courage is an absolute necessity.

Mike McManus presents some shocking statistics in his book, *Marriage Savers*. McManus uses solid research to point out how the American family is splintering. He maintains that the breakup of the family is the central domestic problem of our time, yet the issue has hardly been recognized. Oh, we all nod our heads in assent and cringe when we hear how many marriages are falling apart, but we act as if we can do nothing. McManus cites:

1. *Six out of 10 new marriages are failing. Divorces have tripled since 1960. And before they are 18, three-fifths of children*

will live with a single parent.

2. *Cohabitation has soared sevenfold since 1970. The majority of all marriages in America are preceded by cohabitation. And those who cohabit before marriage increase their odds of divorce by 50 percent.*
3. *Fewer young people are getting married at all. In 1993 there were 42 million adults who had never married—twice the number in 1970 (21 million). The percentage of men ages 30-34 who have never married has tripled from 9 percent to 30 percent.*
4. *Only 55 percent of adults are married today—the lowest figure ever.*
5. *Who gets hurt the most! The innocent—the children.*[5]

Startling statistics to be sure! It is bewildering. We live in the finest of countries—a land of great wealth and prosperity. We have at our disposal every possible technological invention developed to ease our burdens. We have developed drugs to deal with any type of mental or emotional problem we could possibly think of. We have developed new psychological theories used to help people excuse themselves from any type of moral responsibility. Our country is known for its great care, compassion, and concern. Yet we seem to be more miserable than ever before.

But we are resourceful. Rather than screw up the courage to face our real issues—our inability and unwillingness to stay put during difficult times—we pursue our own happiness and pleasure with a vengeance. Catering to every visual or tactile sensation, vicarious thrill, and carnal urge, our culture promises happiness in every measure, for every purse, to every taste. We pursue it till we are weary, but we can never hold it long.

Overcoming Fear

The national pastime today for both men and women is "getting it together." And try as we might to "get it together," we somehow never ever seem to. The quick fixes society and psychology promise us wear off.

In *The Wizard of Oz*, the Cowardly Lion, despite his own fears, placed the well-being of his companions above his own well-being. Although the Lion knew he stood a slim chance of receiving the courage he so desperately longed for, he went ahead on the perilous journey for the sake of his friends. His own needs were secondary to those of his companions. Despite his protest, the Cowardly Lion always acted courageously. Despite his many fears, he did the courageous, heroic thing—he acted in the face of fear.

To act in spite of one's fears requires an incredible amount of courage. Honoré de Balzac, in his book, *Cousin Bette*, describes it beautifully:

> *To achieve fame in art—and in art must be included all the mind's creations—courage, above all, is needed, courage of a kind that the ordinary man has no idea of, which is perhaps described for the first time here. ... To think, to dream, to conceive fine works, is a delightful occupation. ... It means creating, bringing to birth, laboriously rearing the child, putting it to bed every evening gorged with milk, kissing it every morning with a mother's never spent affection, licking it clean, clothing it over and over again in the prettiest garments, which it*

spoils again and again. It means never being disheartened by the upheavals of a frenetic life, but making of the growing work of art a living masterpiece, which in sculpture speaks to all eyes, in literature to all minds, in painting to all memories, in music to every heart. This is the travail of execution. The hand must constantly progress, in constant obedience to the mind. And the ability to create is no more to be commanded at will than love is: both powers are intermittent. ... And work is a fatiguing snuggle, dreaded as well as passionately loved by the fine and powerful natures that are often broken by it. ... If the artist does not throw himself into his work like Curtius into the gulf, like a soldier against a fortress, without counting the cost; and if, once within the breach, he does not labor like a miner buried under a fallen roof; ... then the work remains unfinished, it perishes, is lost within the workshop, where production is impossible, and the artist is a looker—on at his talent's suicide. ... It is for these reasons that the same laurel wreath is bestowed on great poets and great generals.[6]

Courageous men do this all the time—overcome their ordinary fears, desires, and wants to attain greatness by serving some great good. The courageous man tells us that we fail, not by aiming too high in life, but by aiming too low. The courageous man also helps us understand that we are sadly mistaken in supposing that happiness is a right or an end in itself. The courageous man seeks not happiness but goodness, and his fulfillment lies in achieving it.

In Balzac's beautiful statement there is one point with

which I would disagree: "common minds have no conception" of this courage. This is the error, which comes from identifying courage with obviously spectacular acts like the soldier's charge or Michelangelo's struggles in completing the paintings on the ceiling of the Sistine Chapel. To reserve courage only for "heroes" and artists shows how little one knows of the profundity of almost any human being's inner development. Courage is necessary in every step of a person's movement in life. Courage, whether the soldier's courage in risking death or the child's in going off to school, means the power to let go of the familiar and the secure. Courage is required in the hour-to-hour decision to love one another despite the absence of any joyful feelings or in the face of pain-filled emotions such as fear and anger.

When the Cowardly Lion acted in spite of his fears, there was a selfless quality to his behavior and character. He was willing to give himself to others and their well-being. He served others. This is an incredibly helpful picture for those of us who want to be heroes, who desire to act courageously but are unsure what to do. The Cowardly Lion points us to the truth that heroism and courage are found in giving ourselves to others and binding ourselves to them, "for better or worse, richer or poorer, in sickness and in heath, till death do us part." This vow holds true for many relationships other than marriage. We bind ourselves to others. Our lives are marked by our commitment to our family, our spouses, and our children. It is this picture of masculinity that is so desperately needed today.

Will You Stay or Will You Go?

The questions before men today are strong: Will you

remain a real man? Will you wilt? Will you fall apart? Will you cut bait and run? Will you cash in the one thing you have left—your character, the essence of who you are?

These questions must be answered for a change in our world and society to occur. People, events, catastrophes, stock market crashes, and disasters can take things away from you—things on the outside. But no one can ever take away what's on the inside—your heart, soul, character, courage. You can throw it away. But no one can ever *take* it away.

So the question becomes: Will you throw away your courage and your ability to love and stay put when it becomes incredibly difficult? That is the question before every man who desires to be more than what he is. When the marriage turns out differently than you had expected, will you stay put? When things around you are taken away, what will happen on the inside—where you live with yourself? Will your character and courage survive?

Empty Promises

Sadly, in America today, men and their character are not surviving. A man without courage is thus a symptom of contemporary America. Men are facing an affliction of the spirit because their lives have been shaped by the things around them rather than by what is inside them. Men today are embracing a lifestyle based almost entirely on buying and having. Through purchase of bigger and better homes, cars, clothes, vacation retreats, men hope to numb the effects of the real problem—their character, their insides, the essence of what makes a man a man. We are increasingly led to believe that our deepest spiritual needs—the sorts of realities the Bible talks about—can be met simply by buying the right consumer goods.

Some men reading this might discount what I am suggesting. But consider how many of the advertisements on television promise to deliver us the blessings, that upon reflection, we once supposed could come only from right relationships with God and with our neighbors. Closeness, love, relationships, peace, and harmony can all be had by purchasing the right soft drink or using the right toothpaste. We all chuckled at the Anheuser Busch beer commercial where one man, trying to get a beer from his friend says, "I love you, man." And we chuckled because we all know the real love is for the beer and the benefits of having the beer. We somehow believe this beer will deliver far more than what is in the can. We are being told that Budweiser can help us overcome our loneliness and sadness of the soul.

We are trapped on a roller coaster of enthusiasm and dashed hopes. We rush from one fix to the next, following the latest fashions in self-fulfillment. We try pills, sensation, immersion in causes, carnality, the stylish guru, the "mentor," counseling, searching in widening circles for who knows what, ever searching but always afraid. We listen to anyone who promises to relieve our emptiness.

Despite all the surveys that suggest America is "religious," the two thriving religions that never seem to make the list are individualism and hedonism. We like to think we are good, upright, moral, decent people but we are instead a nation of narcissists, driven by our needs.

Freedom of Self

The rise of the self—whatever that self is—is the hallmark

of our culture. And a symptom is the rise of self-image. Self-image is more important than character and the courage to do the right thing. Men learn that the self-image they project counts for more than skills and experience. Men today are judged according to their possessions, their clothes, and their personalities—not, as in previous centuries, by their character. As a result, men have learned to adopt a theatrical view of life. Although it is still good to perform well on the job, more concern is given to superficial impressions and images so the self becomes almost indistinguishable from its surface. What counts is what others think of you rather than what you are and what you think of yourself.

As part of this self-image, men have been taught to believe that their own individual freedom—what they want to do with their lives—is of paramount importance. Today, "freedom of choice" means keeping your options open. And so men enter relationships and life believing they can be anything they want. This, however, now means that who I am can be discarded like a change of clothes. Choices of friends, spouses, and careers are all subject to immediate cancellation. After all, I need my freedom to choose and sometimes my choices impinge on my own personal happiness.

Courageous Men Needed

We cowardly lions need to act in spite of our fears, doubts. and concerns. We need to be moved by courageous deeds and acts rather than by economics and our own personal wants and desires. The economy might help give us things we desire, but it can never touch our souls because, in the final analysis, it cannot tell us what we should be. It can never produce courageous men.

Courageous men tell all of us what life should be. Courageous men are not necessarily presidents, CEOs, or great athletes. Courageous men are those who do not fit the courageous or heroic mold at all, and from whom, perhaps, we should least expect great or heroic deeds. This kind of hero has been with us all along and these men discharge their duties without giving a second thought to fashionable theories of the times. Any of us can be a courageous man! Ordinary people do heroic things every day that are simply unthinkable to the anti-hero concept of life. J.R.R. Tolkien understood these extraordinary powers when he created the *Lord of the Rings* trilogy. In the prelude to the trilogy he wrote that Hobbits "are made small ... mostly to show up, in creatures of very small physical power the amazing and unexpected heroism of ordinary men in a pinch."[7]

The world is in need of cowardly lions. The world is falling apart for lack of courageous men and women. The family is falling apart for lack of men who will stay. Relationships are being destroyed because so many men fail to keep their word. We need men of courage who will act in spite of the fears, the obstacles, the opposition, the pain.

Promises, Promises

The world desperately needs ordinary men to do extraordinary things on a daily basis—things such as keeping their word and loving their families. It is the little things we do for one another—a kind word, a small deed, a thoughtful gesture—that are indeed extraordinary. Lives are changed when we focus on the small things. Marriages need men who are able to do the "small" things; men who are able to make and keep promises. Many of us talk a great deal about character and moral courage. Yet, despite all the talk, our culture also presents an image whereby not keeping your word, sexual indiscretions, and moral laxity are simply part and parcel of a man. The media make light of sexual liaisons between men and women, leveling the playing field by saying all men have affairs. No, they do not! All men do not lie repeatedly to their wives. All men do not cheat on their partners. All men do not quit so easily and walk out on their commitments to family, friends, and loved ones.

The Promise Keepers movement reminds us all of the importance of being good, courageous, moral men. Despite the many theological discussions surrounding Promise Keepers, by the power of the Word of God, the movement has helped many men realize that making and keeping promises is something good and God-pleasing. God Himself makes promises—covenants—with His sinful people. All the Scriptures hang on a promise—that God is love and He will love His people into life. The Scriptures are full of covenants, unconditional promises God makes to His people. And so a man's promise contains incredible power. Lewis Smeades said, "When a man makes a promise, he creates an island of certainty in a heaving ocean of uncertainty ... when you make a promise you have created a small sanctuary of trust within the jungle of unpredictability."[8]

One's vow creates the only unconditional bond that withstands the acids of time and change. Casey and I were married in 1986. I thought that if anyone could make a marriage go, it would be me. I was a pastor, after all, and working on a graduate degree in counseling. We entered the marriage on November 1, 1986, and by December 25 of that same year we both thought our lives were ruined. We had no idea what marriage would be like. Oh, we had some thoughts, but the reality was incredibly different. As time marched on, we had no inkling what having three children would do to our lives—the joys as well as the sorrows. We never dreamt of the incredible pain we would experience when one of our children was hurt. The stress of my ministry and pursuing a Ph.D. brought enormous amounts of pressure upon our lives and our marriage. And when we stood together on that November afternoon, we couldn't have guessed a tenth of what was going to happen to us.

But the truth is, we didn't need to. We made a promise. We recited a vow. Of all the people Casey and I had dated, we chose each other. I have often asked students in my pastoral counseling courses, "Do you think you could have found a better mate than the one you have?" I get rude looks and glares. But I think it important to say that there are always going to be "better" people out there than me. I know there are better-looking men, smarter men, funnier men, gentler men than me. But it doesn't matter. Because in all the world, Casey and I said before God and His church that we have chosen this one to love and to adore. Our words bind us to each other. There may be better-looking, smarter, or funnier women than Casey, although I find that hard to believe. But not for me. Casey is the one I've chosen to love and adore and she has done the same for me.

I still believe that despite the enormous divorce statistics, we all hope this is true regarding marriage. We still long for a sense of faithfulness and fidelity among people—if not ourselves, then maybe the couple taking their wedding vows. We still cling to marriage with a romantic affection. We cry at weddings because we can scarcely bear the beauty of the union we are witnessing—and also because hard experience has taught us of its fragility. We marry out of hope, or fear, or desire, or desperation, and certainly out of love; and yet I believe that in every marriage, no matter how begun, there is that kernel of possibility that this is the one for the ages.

You can't know what you're getting into when you get married. A man or woman can change and become several different people before a marriage is finished. But so what? The vow literally means that when a man makes a promise, he stretches himself out into circumstances that no one can control and he controls at least one thing: he will be there no matter what the circumstances turn out to be.

I have been stressing the importance of men keeping their word in marriage because I believe it is the most important social institution there is in our world. But the point must not be missed that real men are courageous by simply keeping their word. Period. When we speak, we mean what we say. When we say we will stay, we stay and work on that which has been given to us.

Despite all the ups and downs of being raised in my family, the one thing I learned from my father was staying power. To be sure, our family wasn't perfect. There were fights and squabbles and things were not as they should have been. But we knew Dad would come home. We knew that one way or another, he would be there for his family. Dad stayed and stayed and stayed. He worked long hours on the road, traveling the state of Michigan so his wife and four sons could be provided for. He hated his job but he kept at it because he needed to provide for his family. In many ways I didn't appreciate his staying power until I took on a family of my own. We take one another and our families for granted so easily. We treat one another as if we are throw-away people. We love to have people around when we are in the mood, but once our needs are met, we discard them like so much refuse. I thank God for my dad who, in his own inimitable way, stayed put for all of us. He endured. He held fast.

For Christian men, our courage doesn't come from telling ourselves, "I think I can, I think I can, I think I can." We are not the little engine that could. Rather, courage comes from our close personal walk with our Lord Jesus Christ. And our ability to stay comes from precisely the reality that we have a God who stayed for us even unto death—death on a cross. When Jesus could have turned away from the cross, He stayed on course, setting His face toward Jerusalem and Golgotha. When He could have come down from the cross and sidestepped the suffering, He stayed. When He could have summoned armies of angels to deliver Him and could have called down air strikes on His adversaries, He stayed. He persevered and stayed all the way until that moment when He cried out, "It is finished."

And He did it because He's a God of love, a God of His Word, a God who stays. He did it so we too might be men of love, men of our word, men who stay. He did it so we too might be transformed into the image of His dear Son. He did it so, come what may, nothing will ever separate us from our God and the ones He has given us to love—our families.

6 *There's No Place like Home*

THE JOURNEY TOWARD CONTENTMENT

In the Wizard of Oz, Dorothy left friends and family for a place "somewhere over the rainbow." She ran away from the very ones who loved her and who could help her find her real home. She thought that in some place other than her ordinary home, she could find the happiness and contentment she always longed for. It wasn't until her grand adventure in Oz, where she confronted—or rather was confronted by—witches and haunted forests and flying monkeys, that she finally discovered "there's no place like home." Glinda, the Good Witch of the North, asks her as she believes she is stranded in Oz forever, "What have you learned?" Dorothy responds, "There's no place like home," and then clicks her heels three times and magically finds herself back in the safety of her bed.

There's No Place like Home

In *The Birth of Tragedy from the Spirit of Music*, Nietzsche spoke of our hunger, our all-consuming longing for home. Surely he is right: all of us have a powerful hunger for home. We search till we exhaust ourselves from searching to find a place we can call home. And, of course, like Dorothy, so many of us seem to believe that home is someplace else, somewhere else over the rainbow where we can finally discover what we have always longed for.

So what is home? Where is home? Frederick Buechner says that "the word *home* brings to mind before anything else ... a place, and in its fullest sense not just the place where you happen to be living at the time, but a very special place with very special attributes which make it clearly distinguishable from all other places. The word *home* summons up a place—more specifically a house within that place—which you have rich and complex feelings about, a place where you feel, or did feel once, uniquely at *home*, which is to say a place where you feel you belong and which in some sense belongs to you, a place where you feel that all is somehow ultimately well even if things aren't going all that well at any given moment."[9] For most of us, to think about home eventually leads us to think back to our childhood homes, the place where our lives started, the place which, off and on throughout our lives, we keep going back to—if only in dreams and memories. This image of home is apt to determine the kind of place, perhaps a place inside yourself, you spend the rest of your life searching for, even if you are not aware that you are searching. I even suspect that those who as children never had such a place in actuality, had instead some kind of dream of such a home, which for them played an equally crucial role. It is this kind of home so many men live their lives hoping to find.

It may sound surprising when I say, on the basis of my own clinical practice as well as that of my professional colleagues, that the chief problem of many men today is an inability to find a place they can call *home*. Call it emptiness or what you will, many men are lost. Just as a young child is dazed and confused when he can't find his way home, so today, men appear to be dazed and confused and empty. By that I mean not only that many men do not know what they want; they often do not have any clear idea of what they feel. When they talk about their lives, about their lack of individuality, or lament their inability to make important decisions, it soon becomes evident that their underlying problem is that they haven't a clue what they are really searching for. As the book of James says, they are "like a wave of the sea, blown and tossed by the wind" (James 1:6).

They feel swayed this way and that, with painful feelings of powerlessness. The complaint which leads them to come for help may be, for example, that their love relationships always break up or that they cannot go through with marriage plans or are dissatisfied with the marriage partner. But they do not talk long before they make it clear that they expect the marriage partner, real or hoped-for, to fill some lack, some vacancy within themselves; and they are anxious and angry because she doesn't meet their every need.

What Do You Want?

Many men generally can talk fluently about what they *should* want—to complete their college degrees successfully, to get a job, to fall in love, marry and raise a family—but it is soon evident, even to them, that they are describing what others—parents, professors, bosses—expect of them rather than what they themselves want. These men live their lives based on the expectations of others and never seem to come to an understanding of what their own real wants and needs are. Some men realize that they are a collection of mirrors, reflecting what everyone else expects of them. There appears to be no internal direction to their lives because they have never figured out what they really want.

Rather than longing to be heroes, to do something outstanding, these men simply want to "fit in." They live their lives as though they are directed by radar fastened to their heads, perpetually telling them what other people expect of them. These men get their motives and directions from others.

I am not suggesting that godly men should focus solely on themselves and their wants, goals, needs, and dreams irrespective of commitments to their family. I am not suggesting that a man's own wants should supersede the clear direction of the Word of God. I am suggesting, however, that men need to figure out what really makes them tick. There is a place for appropriate and healthy introspection. Men need to figure out what it is that drives them; what their fears, joys, sorrows, and concerns are. Men need to be able to step back and come to terms with who they are, how they have been influenced by others, and the many issues that continually drive them forward in their lives.

Instead of recognizing that their real longing is for a place where they are loved unconditionally, a place they can call home, many men mistakenly pursue happiness as a substitute goal. Despite the fact that we are now healthier and grow to be older; that even the least affluent among us are surrounded by material luxuries undreamed of even a few decades ago; and regardless of all the stupendous scientific knowledge we can summon at will, men often end up feeling that their lives have been wasted, that instead of being filled with happiness, their years were spent in anxiety and boredom.

Where Is the Passion?

Kierkegaard wrote, "Let others complain that the time is evil; I complain that it is wretched; for it is without passion. People's thoughts are thin and frail like lace; they are themselves pitiable like the lacemakers. The thoughts of their hearts are too wretched to be sinful. For a worm it might be considered sinful to entertain such thoughts, but not for men made in the image of God. Their pleasures are solemn and inert, their passions sleepy. They perform their duties, these shopkeeper souls; but even so they permit themselves, like the Jews, to clip the coin a little bit. They think that even if our Lord keeps ever so accurate records they can still fool Him somewhat. Fie on them! That is why my soul always returns to the Old Testament and to Shakespeare. There one still feels that it is people who speak; they hate someone, they love someone, they murder their enemies, they curse their enemies' descendants through all generations, they sin."[10]

We seem to lack passion even today. We seem to be hollow men with nothing that compels us or drives us into the lives of others. Ours is an increasingly passionless generation. And a huge part of the problem is that our culture no longer provides the moral examples, heroic roles, vocational challenges that are worthy of who we are as God's forgiven, redeemed people. Many men have lost their vitality and enthusiasm because there is no longer much about which they can become authentically excited. We have reduced the world and truth to mere clichés that no longer have any power or influence over our lives.

And because our lives seem too empty and passionless, we search for happiness in all the wrong places. Happiness is not something that simply happens. It is not the result of good fortune or random chance. It is not something money can buy or power command. It does not depend upon outside events, but rather on how we interpret them. Happiness, in fact, is a condition that must be prepared for, cultivated, and defended privately by each person. Men who learn to control inner experience will be able to determine the quality of their lives, which is as close as any of us can come to being happy.

Yet we cannot reach happiness by consciously searching for it. Ask yourself whether you are happy and you cease to be so. It is by being fully involved with every detail of our lives, pursuing God's plan and will for our lives, that we can be happy and fulfilled men and women. Viktor Frankl, the Jewish psychiatrist, summarized it beautifully in his book, *Man's Search for Meaning*. "Don't aim at success—the more you aim at it and make it a target, the more you are going to miss it. For success, like happiness, cannot be pursued; it must ensue ... as the unintended side-effect of one's personal dedication to a cause greater than oneself. "[11]

Over the Rainbow

So, however will we find that place somewhere over the rainbow? How can we find our real longing and yearning for meaning, purpose, and existence? How can we find a place we can really call home?

To be sure, our lives as men are the outcome of many forces that shape our experience. In earlier chapters, we looked at the many masculine stereotypes that influence who we are as men. Most of these forces are outside our control. There is not much we can do about our looks, our temperament, or our constitution. We cannot decide—at least so far—how tall we will grow, how smart we will get. We can choose neither our parents nor time of birth, and it is not in your power or mine to decide whether there will be a war or a depression. The instructions contained in our genes, the pull of gravity, the pollen in the air, the historical period into which we are born—these and innumerable other conditions determine what we see, how we feel, what we do. It is not surprising that so many men believe that their fate is primarily determined by outside forces.

Yet we have all experienced times when, instead of being buffeted by anonymous forces, we do feel in control of our actions, masters of our own fate. On the rare occasions when that happens, we feel a sense of exhilaration, a deep sense of enjoyment that is long-cherished and that becomes a landmark in our memory for what life should be like.

Look back at what Viktor Frankl said. Frankl wrote his best-selling book, *Man's Search for Meaning*, while he was imprisoned in Nazi concentration camps. Frankl learned that the Nazis were able to take many things from the prisoners. They could take your family and murder them in front of your very eyes. They could take your possessions, your home, and all you held dear in life. They could torture you until you were unable to stand any more pain. Though they inflicted these atrocities upon people, the one thing they knew they could never steal from an individual was his ability to choose his attitude. Frankl writes, "They hated us for it." Try as the Nazis might to dehumanize the prisoners, which made it easier to abuse them, the prisoners in Frankl's hut refused to lose the dignity of being human. They were able to transcend the most horrible of times because of their ability to choose right over wrong, humanness over the demonic, kindness over hatred, and mercy and compassion over evil. Frankl points out that people who have survived concentration camps or who have lived through near-fatal physical dangers, often recall that in the midst of their ordeal they experienced extraordinarily rich epiphanies in response to such simple events as hearing the song of a bird in the forest, completing a hard task, or sharing a crust of bread with a fellow prisoner.

Contrary to what we usually believe, the best moments in our lives are not the passive, receptive, relaxing times—although such experiences can also be enjoyable, if we have worked hard to attain them. The best moments usually occur when a person's body or mind is stretched to its limits in a voluntary effort to accomplish something difficult and worthwhile. In other words, we make it happen. For a child, it could be grabbing a bat, standing up to the plate and, despite the fear of being hit, digging in, watching the ball, and hitting it with all his might; for a swimmer it could be trying to beat his own record; for a violinist, mastering an intricate musical passage; and for a man, it could be discovering and making his own family, life, and home a place where his contentment and delight are found.

These experiences are not necessarily pleasant when they occur. Sometimes the swimmer's muscles ache during his most memorable race, his lungs feel like exploding, and he is dizzy with fatigue—yet these could be the best moments of his life. Sometimes for men, living in a relationship with conflict, with children who constantly demand attention, can seem unbearable at the time. Some men have said to me in therapy, "I can't do it." They even use God as an excuse, saying, "The Lord certainly wouldn't want me to remain unhappy, would He?" Sometimes, I have been tempted to say, "I don't think He really cares." Because in one sense I don't think He does. Oh, to be sure, God wants us to be fully alive. He wants us to experience joy in His kingdom. He even says, "I came that they may have life, and have it to the full" (John 10:10). But this abundant life Jesus talks about is a far cry from mere happiness.

We have been called to a life of forgiveness and grace. God called us to be His people and, because we belong to Him, we are enabled to do great things for God and for others. Doing great things may, at the time, be unpleasant. Doing great things may mean doing small things in relationships, such as remembering to take out the trash and saying "please" and "thank you." Doing great things may mean, even when we least feel like it, completing acts of kindness and love. Our lives are never to be determined by the fleeting fancy of emotions that can be quite deceptive. Our lives, rather, are to be determined by the will of the Lord and how we can show our gratitude and thankfulness to God.

The Realm of Emotions

Feelings simply tell us something is happening in our lives. God never tells us not to feel. He doesn't suggest we should ignore our feelings. We can certainly acknowledge them or pretend they do not exist. We can choose to express or not to express them. But the real issue for all of us becomes what we do with our emotions. We are incapable of changing our emotions directly. God acknowledges that each of us will feel a certain inner longing, maybe even emptiness.

And so we acknowledge our emotions before the Lord. But the attitude with which we acknowledge each kind of emotion is different. When I experience a non-sinful yet painful emotion, I am to come to the Lord, fully expressing my feelings in humble dependence on His comfort and sufficiency. When I experience sinful emotions, however, I must approach Him with an attitude of contrition and repentance, trusting in His forgiveness and His promise to complete His work begun in me. Practically, this means I should openly experience my unrighteous feelings before God in a humble spirit of confession. This does not consist of superficial prayers such as, “Oh, Lord, please forgive me for being angry." Rather, it is better to cry, “God, I am furious! I am livid with rage. And I know I am wrong. I want to go your way and be filled with your compassion, but right now I am bitter. Please forgive me. I commit myself to your purposes.” By this I mean we must not suppress any emotion, whether by denying its existence or by minimizing its fullness. And for many men, that's a hard concept to grasp.

But there are also times when we can acknowledge our emotions but not express them. I am very concerned when I hear therapists tell clients they need to work through their emotions. First of all, I'm never sure what that is supposed to mean. Second, I think it might mean that heavy emotions need a cathartic experience or they will build up and cause deep psychological harm. Frankly, there is not once shred of psychological or Biblical evidence that warrants such a concern. It is extremely healthy to understand and even verbalize your emotions. It is, however, exceedingly dangerous to make decisions based on your emotions. There is a tremendous danger when men who feel lonely, upset, lost, and confused begin to make decisions based on emotions. There is tremendous havoc wreaked on families and marriages when men, who are in search of their "somewhere over the rainbow" leave their commitments and their relationships to follow their feelings. More problems have arisen for individuals and families in the name of "feelings" than by any other cause. People have justified their behavior based on what they happen to be *feeling*.

When an emotion arises within us, we are to acknowledge it to ourselves and tell God how we feel, allowing ourselves to inwardly experience the full weight of our emotions. And second, we may, at times, need to subordinate the public expression of our feelings as God uses us for His purposes.

Thus, emotional *acknowledgment* is always proper; emotional *expression* may be legitimate only when it does not conflict with our fulfilling God's purpose. I am never free just to get things off my chest (i.e., dumping), if that is mean and cruel and hurts other people. I must freely admit to myself and to my God how I feel, confident that God's justifying grace provides me with His acceptance no matter what my emotions are. I am not to suppress my feelings. I must then evaluate whether expressing my acknowledged feelings to anyone other than God will serve His purpose, and I must control this expression accordingly.

In other words, our emotions, which in and of themselves

are gifts of God like all other gifts need to be submitted to something bigger and greater than our own personal desires. And I would suggest that for Christian men, this means rediscovering how we are all agents of God's love and plan for the church and the world. Because of God in Christ, we have cosmic significance. Our calling as children of God means we have been called to a vocation of ultimate importance. And I would further suggest that this vocation is much more than a career or job. It means discovering within the ordinary events and people of our lives the extraordinariness of them all. We have been duped by our culture, and even by our own personal longing for happiness, into believing that home and contentment are someplace out there far away from where we happen to be. The beauty of Dorothy's discovery is that "home" was at her fingertips all along. All it took was for her to realize that the ones she knew and grew up with were the very ones who could provide the home she so longed for.

Expectations and Commitment

Too many men leave their families in search of this mythical Land of Oz. Too many men are hoping that through grand adventures and experiences, the longing and aching can be numbed and they will finally arrive at the place they can call home. But it never happens because home is never experienced or discovered simply through trying to overcome the ache. We have the home we so desperately long for in the people we have been called to love.

Men need to be challenged to pursue with passion the goals or plans the Lord has laid out for them. For the majority of men in this country, life goals are simple: to survive, to raise children who will in turn survive, and, if possible, to do so with a certain amount of comfort and dignity.

But as soon as these basic problems of survival are solved, merely having enough food and a comfortable shelter is no longer sufficient to make men content. New needs are felt, new desires arise. With affluence and power come escalating expectations, and as our level of wealth and comfort keeps increasing, the sense of well-being we hoped to achieve recedes into the distance.

This paradox of rising expectations suggests that improving the quality of life might be an insurmountable task. To be fair, there is no inherent problem in our desire to escalate our goals, as long as we enjoy the struggle along the way. The problem arises when we are so fixated on what we want to achieve that we cease to derive pleasure from the present. When that happens, we forfeit our chance of contentment.

Though the evidence suggests that many men are caught on this frustrating treadmill of rising expectations, many others have found ways to escape. These are men who, regardless of their material conditions, have been able to improve their lives, who are satisfied, and who have a way of making those around them happy.

These men lead vigorous lives, are open to a variety of experiences, keep learning until the day they die, and have strong ties and commitments to other people and to the world in which they live. They enjoy whatever they do, even if tedious or difficult; they are hardly ever bored, and they can take in stride anything that comes their way. Perhaps their greatest strength is that their lives are *under* control because they are in the control of another—the Lord Jesus Christ.

Is This All There Is?

Dorothy only came to her great realization that there is no place like home because she went through terrible trials and difficulties. Today, many men would look at those obstacles and simply throw in their hats and say it's not worth it. Too many men believe that life should be easy and, when it's not, they lose courage and determination in the face of adversity.

Let's be honest—how many genuinely happy men have you known and met? How many men do you know who enjoy what they are doing, who are reasonably satisfied with their lot, who do not regret the past, and who look to the future with genuine confidence? If Diogenes with his lantern had difficulty finding an honest man twenty-three centuries ago, today he would find it more troublesome to find a happy one.

This general unhappiness is the result of no longer having any absolutes in our lives. Call it dread, terror, free-floating anxiety, but at its heart is a sense that there is no meaning to life and that existence is not worth continuing. Nothing seems to make sense. In the last few generations, the specter of a terrorist attack has added an unprecedented threat to our hope. There no longer seems to be any point to our strivings as humans in this world. We are just forgotten specks drifting in the void. As the words from my high school class song remind us, "All we are is dust in the wind."

As men, passing from the hopeful ignorance of youth into sobering adulthood, we sooner or later face an increasingly nagging question: "Is this all there is?" Childhood can be painful, adolescence confusing, but for most people, behind it all there is the expectation that after one grows up, things will get better. During the years of early adulthood, the future still looks promising, the hope remains that one's goals will be realized. But inevitably the bathroom mirror shows the first white hairs, (or in my case, no hair) and confirms the fact that those extra pounds are not about to leave. Eyesight begins to fail and mysterious pains shoot through the body. Like waiters in a restaurant, placing breakfast settings on the surrounding tables while you are still having dinner, these intimations of mortality plainly communicate the message: your time is up; it's time to move on. When this happens, few people are ready. "Wait a minute, this can't be happening to me. I haven't even begun to live. Where's all that money I was supposed to have made? Where are all the good times I was going to have?"

As this realization slowly sets in, men react to it differently. Some try to ignore it, and renew their efforts to acquire more of the things that were supposed to make life good —bigger cars and homes, more power on the job, a more glamorous lifestyle. They are determined still to achieve the satisfaction that has eluded them. Sometimes this solution works, for a while. Their needs are met for a short time because there is no time to realize that the goal has not come any nearer. But if these men take time out to reflect, the disillusionment returns: after each success it becomes clearer that money, power, status, possessions, a new marriage partner, or getting rid of the old one, do not, by themselves, add one iota to the quality of life.

Other men decide to attack the threatening, symptoms directly. If it's a body going to seed that rings the first alarm, they go on diets, join health clubs, do aerobics, buy an exercise machine, or undergo a hair transplant. If the problem seems to be that nobody pays much attention, they buy books about how to get power or how to make friends, or they enroll in assertiveness training courses and have power lunches. After awhile, however, it becomes obvious that these piecemeal solutions won't work either. No matter how much energy we devote to its care, the body will eventually give out. If we are learning to be more assertive, we might inadvertently alienate our friends. And if we devote too much time to cultivating new friends, we might threaten relationships with our spouses and family. There are just so many dams about to burst and so little time to tend to them all.

Daunted by the futility of trying to keep up with all the demands they cannot possibly meet, some men will surrender and retire gracefully into relative oblivion. Some lose themselves in alcohol or the dream world of drugs. Others lose themselves in myriad sexual escapades, achieving a measure of contentment at least for an evening or two. While exotic pleasures and expensive recreations temporarily take the mind off the basic question, "Is this all there is?" few claim to have found a real answer that way.

The Answer

The only answer for men—and for women for that matter—is to remind ourselves once again of where our home really is. God has taken up residence within us as He has won us to Himself through Christ and His death and resurrection. St. Paul says, "To them God has chosen to make known among the Gentiles the glorious riches of this mystery which is Christ in you, the hope of glory" (Colossians 1:27). He also says that our bodies are the temples of the Holy Spirit. This is not to say that we belong to some kind of new age god but rather that the God who is outside us has declared us to be His forgiven sons and daughters through the death and resurrection of Jesus Christ.

Jesus is asking all of us men to drench our minds and spirits in the knowledge of God's love for us. We are the delight of His smiling eyes, the children of His warm heart. God cares for us more than any mother has ever loved her child. If only we could realize how much we are loved, we would, of course, want to respond in thankfulness to our God. "How can I repay the Lord for all His goodness to me?" the psalmist asks in Psalm 116:12. When our hearts are turned toward our heavenly home, toward our God who has loved us into life, then suddenly, life takes on a sense of cosmic significance. The only answer to the malaise facing men today is a return to who we are in Christ. It is a remembering—remembering our Baptism, remembering our Lord's love, remembering the forgiveness of sins He has won for us in His Son's death and resurrection.

Instead of continually focusing on the problem—how apathetic, listless, and empty many men are—we must focus on the solution, the remedy that is only found in the Gospel. We are not to bemoan the problem but to rejoice in the remedy our Lord has given us. Apathy is the natural condition of sinful humanity. We need to concentrate on what can awaken men from their lethargy to become enthusiastic people where they are. We need to help men realize that the answer to their search for home is not in abandoning their commitments and relationships but rather in staying where they are and being used by the Lord to do great things for Him and for others. We need to help men become intensely concerned about their world, their friends, their spouses, their children, and their God. The apostle Paul considers such "aliveness" evidence of the grace of God:

Because of His great love for us, God, who is rich in mercy, made us alive with Christ even when we were dead in transgressions—it is by grace you have been saved. And God raised us up with Christ and seated us with Him in the heavenly realms in Christ Jesus, in order that in the coming ages He might show the incomparable riches of His grace, expressed in His kindness to us in Christ Jesus. Ephesians 2:4-7

Deadness of the spirit need not be the subjective condition of those who live as men in this present age. Vitality, love for life, and a passionate lifestyle stand diametrically opposed to what has become a common emotional condition of many men who seem to have nothing to live for. Jesus came, died, and conquered the powers of darkness, not just to ensure us of a life of everlasting bliss after death, but also to use us in the world to make a lasting difference. When we wonder what to do in our marriages, with our kids, with our jobs, there is little doubt that more than anything else God wants us to recognize each of these persons and situations as opportunities to serve Him with all that we are. God wants to use us as His mouthpieces, His hands, feet, and arms. And He desires that we be used by Him in the most intimate and, at times, the most humdrum and ordinary circumstances—with our spouse, kids, and friends. Our search for the "somewhere over the rainbow" can stop right at our own front doors. Our search for meaning and purpose can end when we look at those around us and realize that in this moment, beginning with today, we can begin to live our lives as acts of love to those around us. That makes life challenging and thrilling.

We speak in such grand terms about accomplishing noble deeds and tasks for our world. We talk about giving our lives in service to some magnificent task and we seldom realize that the task may simply be to love those around us in the most profound way possible. Every moment can become a holy moment. Every relationship can become a holy relationship as God's love in Christ is lived out and actualized among us. It becomes a relatively easy thing to speak of "love" in an abstract manner. Who doesn't love from a distance? But to love up close and personal—now that is a different story. And it is the story we have been given. God in Christ loved us up close and personal. He took upon Himself the story of our lives. He took upon Himself our faults, sins, and failures, and loved us even unto death—up close and personal. Through Him and in His name, we have our "somewhere over the rainbow." Who would have ever dreamed it possible? We have eternal life now. We have hope now. We have passion now. We have the very God of creation and redemption and sanctification dwelling in our midst and our lives. He has called us from an apathetic and listless life to one of grand adventure in His name.

7 *Obstacles along the Journey*

BEYOND JOB TITLES, DEGREES, AND INCOME

In the Wizard of Oz, Dorothy and company encounter a variety of obstacles on their journey: the witch, the poison poppies, flying monkeys, obstinate guards at the Emerald City. All were attempts to keep them from their ultimate goal: finding their hearts' desire. Although our obstacles are different, they can be almost as deadly—not so much physically, but spiritually and psychologically. One of the main obstacles many men face as they make their journey to the Emerald City is an all-consuming passion for their careers. Although careers are indeed blessings from God, like any of God's gifts, they can be converted and transformed into something evil. Many men win their identity primarily through their careers. Their status, income, and ability to exercise power over others are all wrapped up in their careers. In fact, the career is usually the means whereby male identity and self-esteem are achieved.

When a man meets a stranger at a party, usually the first question asked of him is, "What do you do for a living?" People evaluate him and define his social significance when they learn about his job. Since an individual's self-concept is based largely on what he thinks others think of him, such a definition of social significance has great importance.

Because the male's social identity is so tied to his job, he often forgets that there can be a difference between who a person is and what he does. Who a person is usually is so much deeper and more significant than what he does that knowing his occupation may give only a hint of his true identity. But we have been socialized to become "workers." We were taught that having a good job means having a good life. Our jobs are a big part of our lives—there is no denying it. The question is, how much does a man's job dominate his identity? Has your job become your identity?

How Important Is Your Career?

Some men have a healthy balance between career and personal life. They recognize the importance of career but also know that relationships have an equally—if not more-important place in their lives. But there are other men who are workaholics, addicted to their jobs. Their entire identity is a result of the rush of the job, not of their self-esteem. These men feel good about themselves only when they are working, and they have few interests outside work. Workaholic men also heavily identify with a narrow male image. They equate their worth with their paycheck.

Still other men see their jobs as a source of power, intrigue, and excitement—feelings they believe they could not find elsewhere. These men have a strong desire to keep their occupation totally separate from their family, and it is not uncommon for their partners to complain that they think more about their job than their family. These men are seduced by their jobs and led astray from other responsibilities. They relate to work as to a mistress, willing to do anything to please it and revealing a part of themselves in the job that no one else ever sees. It seems their job brings out their passion and they only feel alive when they are working. They think their job understands them. It meets their needs. Though their partners might realize they aren't having *actual* affairs, it certainly feels as if they are.

Most men derive a great deal of satisfaction and self-esteem from their work. I like to accomplish things and I am proud of my accomplishments. When I was originally working on this book, for example, it was an immense thrill. I would come home from my study at the seminary and say to my wife, "Look, Dear, look what I did today." I'm like a little kid when it comes to my performance and I want my wife to notice me. The problem again is not the work. The problem is when a man's work is his only source of self-esteem. Many men work hard because their entire sense of self is consumed with what they do and how well they perform.

And most men are capable of working all the time. There is always more to do. There is always one more task at the office. There will always be compliments paid and accolades given when a man continues to keep long hours at the office. But it is never enough.

When we realize that our accomplishments aren't enough, we face a choice. We can work even harder to see if that will fill the void, or we can look for other things to add meaning to our lives. It is difficult for men to find worth outside of their work. In order to do this, we must expand our perception of ourselves and of the things that lend meaning to our lives.

How Can I Use You?

Christian men should know better than to evaluate the significance of a person totally in terms of his career. We are supposed to be people who do not live according to our sinful nature but according to the Spirit. This means we do not use the same criteria society does to evaluate individuals. Unfortunately, Christians do not always live in accord with the Word of God. In an overwhelming number of churches, the tendency is to evaluate people in much the same way the secular world evaluates them.

Imagine the following example. A husband and wife begin to attend a local church. They visit one Sunday and are met by the official greeters of the church. The greeters surround the new couple and begin to ask questions: "What's your name?" "Where do you live?" "Where are you from?" And finally, "What do you do?"

If the man answers that he is a local elementary school principal, you can almost imagine what will happen. Immediately the greeters call over the Sunday school superintendent or Bible class leader and whisper that the man is a principal and teacher. A quick prayer goes up, "Thank You, God! I've got another warm body for that class!" And before the conversation ends, someone says, "We sure hope you can come back and worship with us because we sure could use you."

The man's career has been the basis for evaluation and he has been approved because he can be used in the work of the church. No one knows if he is a Christian and a committed disciple of the Lord Jesus Christ and has a firm grasp on the Scriptures.

Erich Fromm once said that the problem with our age is

that we love things and use people instead of using things and loving people. Maybe the church could take a page from the writings of this great humanist. We should be considering people in terms of how we can love them, not in terms of how we might use them.

I find it delightful that when Jesus chose His disciples, He never once required that they be the elite in society. He did not choose twelve men who held prestigious positions in society. Instead, he chose a couple of fishermen, a tax collector, and two troublemakers who were called the "sons of thunder."

Jesus looked within people and tried to discern their hungers, dreams, and values. Jesus also knew that regardless of their personalities and disposition, He could use them in service to His kingdom. Jesus knew that these men from various backgrounds could serve Him in unique ways, because He had called them. The issue was and continues to be the One calling, not the one being called.

The Meaning of Life

Jesus also knows that many people who are impressed with certain careers are also hollow and superficial. On the other hand, many men whose job status is not highly ranked by society prove to possess greatness of spirit and character, which makes them great people to know.

When I was in the tenth grade at St. Johns high school in the small town of St. Johns, Michigan, I had my first course in biology. Mr. Jehoski, our teacher, was incredibly motivating and humorous. His classes usually filled up immediately, so I thought I was privileged to be part of his first-year biology class. I remember one of his assignments was for us to write a paper on the meaning of life. I was excited about this opportunity to finally make public my understanding of my relationship with Jesus Christ and what that meant for my life and for the world. I was a committed Christian, actively involved in evangelism in my local church, and I saw this paper as a grand opportunity to share my faith.

I remember looking at my paper—completely covered with red ink—in shock and horror. Mr. Jehoski laughed at my ideas of a personal God who had revealed Himself in His Son Jesus Christ. He particularly laughed at the suggestion that my goal in life was to be a pastor. Although respected in other arenas, in my sophomore biology class I was ridiculed by the teacher who said, "Why don't you consider doing something really worth-while?"

As a student in a public high school I learned early on how the world views things differently than Christians. My biology teacher was impressed with a big, important job that could bring in a lot of money. He certainly wasn't impressed with a young high school student who had his heart bent on service.

It is so very important that Christian men impress upon their children and loved ones that as Christians, being successful people is more important than having prestigious careers. Christians know that it is possible to have a deep sense of value, even when the world is unimpressed. And the reverse is also true: it is possible for people to amaze the world with their accomplishments but inwardly feel like failures.

What's a Career Worth?

In my own counseling practice, I have discovered that the

all-consuming nature of pursuing a career brings many men to very difficult crossroads in their lives. Men who have been raised believing that work brings happiness arrive at a time when they begin to ask, "Is this all there is?" Perhaps the rapid success of promotions of a man's earlier years has slowed down and now he feels he is not going anywhere. As he watches the younger people in his profession who seem to be moving ahead of him, he knows he is no longer viewed as the promising executive. Rather, he has become an established bureaucrat, nervously protecting his job against the assaults of the young "upstarts." These men come to therapy having their self-confidence shattered and broken.

These men often develop resentment toward many people. Feeling threatened and hurt, they react with pettiness, attaching great importance to every symbol of prestige. The size of another man's desk, the kind of office equipment he has, the location of his office, the amount of secretarial help—all can take on exaggerated importance.

Even clergymen face these issues. Some pastors in their forties and fifties wonder if they will ever be called to serve a big parish. Some pastors work in small congregations, making small salaries with few pats on the back for a job well done. It is not uncommon for these pastors to begin to compare themselves to former classmates to see how they stack up. Sadly, many pastors who don't stack up too well begin to call into question their competence and abilities. The size of the congregation and the numbers in worship become an all-consuming passion for a pastor who wants to make it big. Instead of being faithful, he pushes himself to become successful—at least in terms of the world. Of course, it is not wrong for pastors to want their churches to grow and increase in size and attendance. That is certainly God's will. But the fact remains that the Lord is the One who grows the church and there are times when a pastor is doing all he can as the Lord's servant in that specific locale and the parish may not grow. If his identity is based on a standard of success defined by the world, he is going to be in sad shape.

Other men are threatened when their greatest fears are realized—their jobs are phased out. When men in their forties and fifties suddenly find that their services are no longer required, their egos are shattered and their self-confidence is gone. Often their personal wealth is diminished and they see little left to live for.

It is hard for a man who has lost his job not to feel contempt for himself. He sold himself to the demands of the job, tailoring his personality to the expectations of his role. He compromised his personal integrity in order to fit the expectations of the company. He said the right things, held the proper political views, attended the right church, and joined the right country club in his effort to establish the proper image. He became what he thought his company wanted, and he feels betrayed.

Fortunately, most men do not lose their jobs during their prime earning years. But even those who remain employed often find their jobs increasingly meaningless and come home emotionally dissipated at the end of the day. That exhaustion is not from physical exertion but from the emotional emptiness of not doing anything that seems worthwhile.

Obstacles in the Road

To deal with these obstacles, men choose a variety of

escape routes. Some men become heavy drinkers. Hard work and hard drinking go hand in hand for many men; alcoholism is often rationalized as just another occupational hazard. It is easier for men to deny they have a drinking problem when they can rationalize it as part of their job: "Everyone drinks and it is expected of you." True. Many businessmen are expected to make deals over martini lunches; a bottle of alcohol is considered an appropriate male gift.

Men can find every reason in the world to drink and numerous ways to rationalize the drinking. Are things slowly slipping away at work, but you don't want to face it? These are tough issues and they are hard to face. But men need to come to terms with these problems if things are ever to change for the better.

Another escape route for men consumed by their careers is to pursue the career even harder. If men find themselves measuring their worth by the size of their paycheck, then they will continue to work long hours. Do you justify long hours, stomach problems, and family tension because you are making money? I'm not talking about making enough money to live on, but rather pursuing money for the sake of money. We have been led to believe that our worth is in our wallets. Ironically, the harder we work, the more narrowly our worth becomes defined. We value ourselves less as we value money more. And our value to others begins to drop as well. If we give our all to only one thing, we seldom have anything or anyone left—including ourselves. When the job becomes everything to us, we must become everything to the job. When the job becomes everything, we believe we are worth nothing.

The fact remains that men try a number of other escape

routes to deal with jobs going nowhere. I will address other escape routes later in the book, but the main problem is that too many men define success by virtue of their job or their career.

Beyond the Career

Jesus puts emphasis on the little things we do in love rather than the big things that impress other people. We are His forgiven children; Jesus is not impressed by our job titles, degrees, or level of income. Jesus simply desires that His redeemed children reach out in love to one another. Whether we are bakers, farmers, or candlestick makers, Jesus calls us to love one another. In small acts of kindness and deeds done out of love for the Father, Jesus is pleased. Many Christian men have found success in taking advantage of opportunities to express love in simple ways. It is more important to express love in the little things daily than to gain fame in the eyes of the world. Christians believe that if we are faithful in these small things, we can also be faithful in great things. We also know that even as Jesus came not to be served, but to serve, and give His life as a ransom for many, so we too are considered great as we stoop to serve those around us.

8 *The Journey of Fatherhood*

SETTING OUR EYES ON THE HEAVENLY FATHER

My Father grew up in the upper peninsula of Michigan during the depression and World War II. He was a good-looking, tough-minded Finn. Having parents who immigrated from Finland, my father was raised to work hard, play hard, and keep a stiff upper lip. He met and married my mother, who worked in Traverse City, Michigan. When I was a child, my father worked for the state of Michigan as a health screening technician. He was gone almost every week, examining and testing state employees from various parts of the state. My father was rigid in his beliefs about race, women, and men.

I was his fourth child, the younger of twins by six minutes. Although Dad was gone on the road a lot, he tried to do things that showed all of us boys he loved us. Dad and Mom bought a cottage in Marion, Michigan, about two hours north of our home in Lansing. Dad took us to the cottage and taught us to fish. We walked down to the river; he hooked my line, sat beside me waiting for a strike, and then helped me take the fish off the hook. He untangled the line, and chased away unwelcome critters. There were times we just enjoyed being together.

I remember when I was about twelve years old, Mom and Dad had company over—Don and Leona—good friends of the family. They were playing cards in the kitchen, and my twin brother and I were ready for bed. We brushed our teeth, put on our pajamas, and proceeded downstairs to kiss Mom and Dad goodnight. It was a regular bedtime ritual. I went to Mom and gave her a kiss goodnight, then moved toward Dad to kiss him on the cheek. As I approached, my father leaned back and said words I will never forget, "Don't you think you are getting a bit old for this?" I was stunned. It had never dawned on me that I would ever be too old to kiss my father. But the world had changed. Suddenly, I was aware that a time would come when father and sons were no longer supposed to act a particular way. And from that moment on, I knew that it was okay to shake Dad's hand, but not okay to show him love by giving him a kiss on the cheek.

And from that point on, I knew my father wasn't quite what I expected. Now, as a father myself, I realize my expectations weren't realistic. I was much like the characters in *The Wizard of Oz*. The Wizard was perceived to be all-powerful, the great beneficent Oz. He was perceived by some to be the ultimate father-figure, provider, protector of the Emerald City. Once the curtain was pulled back, however, and the man was exposed, Dorothy and company saw him for who he was: a small, frail, balding man. At times, we put our fathers in the same position.

We expect them to be all-powerful. When they fail—as they will as sinful men—we think they aren't good fathers. As we make our journey, we need to remind ourselves that being a father may not include the power and spectacle of being a wizard, but it is even better than being a wizard. There is a yearning in all of us for a father who loves and protects us. That role can only be served by our Father God.

The Behavior Rules

My father, like many fathers today, was taught that certain behaviors were considered acceptable for boys, other behaviors were not. Male stoicism, emotional shutdown, and the bread-winner ethic defined manhood. Demonstrating affection, love, nurturance, and care was strictly in the realm of mothers. Dad raised me to serve a system that equates manhood with success, femininity with emotion and nurturance. He thus taught me to shut off a part of who I am—my feelings. As a result of that education, I learned early on to hide away a part of who I am in every other significant relationship. I have always been driven to be liked by people. I have always had a passionate intensity to be loved by others. And although I believe that I was loved, I also know that my relationship with my father could have been much deeper and richer. People have asked me, "Don't you know your dad loved you?" And I have always responded, "Yes, I do." But I also know that our relationship could have been so much better if we could have talked about where we were and how we were together. So much more could have taken place if somehow I could have connected emotionally with my father.

Dad was always larger than life for me. His influence even to this day is dramatic. With only a look, he could give me approval or stop me dead in my tracks. His silence spoke volumes. My dad was a man of great emotions—although I would be hard pressed to figure them out. My dad was also a man of many contradictions and secrets. He wanted to be close, but kept us at a distance. He had anger, but wouldn't tolerate it in others. Even as his physical body declined, his emotional influence continued to grow. My dad was love, anger, rage, compassion, education, confusion, and strength.

The Father's Role

Fathers are the most emotionally powerful people in most men's lives. Emotions between fathers and sons run from love to hate or somewhere in between. You can move halfway across the country, but you can never seem to move away from your father's emotional influence. Whether the influence was positive or negative, who your dad was and is stays with you throughout your life. There is something about your dad that makes him like no other person.

One reason some dads distance themselves from their children emotionally is because they feel unimportant. They have been taught that moms are the ones who need to "be there" for the children. Dad's role is to have a job; he brings home the bacon and mom fries it up. Some men believe that a mother can supply all the nurturance and sustenance children need. But this is simply wrong: a child notices whether or not his father is present, both physically and emotionally.

Dads play a vital role in the child's normal development. Dads safeguard and nurture their child's sense of self and self-respect. Dads help children master their own emotional life and give them appropriate ways to deal with emotional issues. Can you remember standing next to your dad or having your dad walk up and stand next to you? He didn't have to say a word; his mere presence conveyed approval or disapproval. His hand on your shoulder was worth more than a thousand trophies. When I played basketball, during the pre-game I constantly scanned the crowd in hopes of seeing my dad. If he was there, all was well. If not, then it felt like something was missing.

The influence of fathers is universal. If we sat down and made a list of sayings and behaviors common among our dads, I'll bet we'd find many similarities. Can't you just hear our fathers telling us:

- *"Come on, be a man."*
- *"Big boys don't cry."*
- *"I'll give you something to cry about."*
- *"You think your principal was tough, you ain't seen nothing yet, young man."*
- *"As long as you live under my roof you live by my rules."*

Despite this influence, it seems many of us don't even know our dads. We want to know them. We want closeness. We desire intimacy but are never sure we can get it from them. We don't even know how to approach them to ask for anything more because we aren't sure what we are looking for. In fact, as I have met with men, it seems that we all have stories about our dads. But as we talk about our fathers, we seem more confused and mystified.

Connecting Emotionally

It is not easy to reach our dads emotionally, even when we feel the same emotions, because we don't know how to bridge the silence. Instead, we usually settle for communication about common topics and behaviors. We get together over a beer—

alcohol is the social lubricant for many men. We talk about basketball or football or baseball—the “safe” subjects—because they don't really involve anything personal. It is difficult to talk about common feelings, but many sons try to reach their fathers through their behaviors and hope they can make a much needed emotional connection.

Did you ever try to please your dad through your actions? Were you really trying to gain recognition for your accomplishment, or were you hoping for an emotional response? Did you ever do what you thought he wanted and then feel it still wasn’t enough? Maybe you settled for basketball or work talk, because without these there would be no talking at all. After having earned two master's degrees, I still was driven to succeed and make my father proud of my accomplishments. Although there were many reasons I pursued a Ph.D., one main reason was to have my father say the words I so longed to hear, “I am so proud of you, son." I used my accomplishments to connect with my father. I hoped to feel an emotional closeness.

The Joys and Pitfalls of Fatherhood

Today, as the father of three children, it is increasingly apparent that my most treasured "possessions," next to life in Christ, are the members of my family. I share the universal dad reflex that if a fire broke out, after getting the kids safely out of the house, I would go back for the pictures, the scrapbooks, the birthday cards, and notes.

Someday when all is gone, when I can no longer see or hear or talk—when I may no longer know their names—the faces of my loved ones will remain etched on my soul.

I share this because my father, who has passed on, and my family, including my beloved mother, are the most important people in my life. I share this because regardless of all the blunders my father and I made, the one thing that lasted was our love. Regardless of what happened in the past, I am very much like my father, not only because we have the same personality traits, but because we both are sinners. My father and I had issues and problems and difficulties that were never completely resolved. But one thing is certain: all of us are in need of forgiveness. And if our relationships are going to be top priority, then we must do everything within our power to let go of the past, forgive our dads for trying to be what they never could be —perfect—and get on with the business of our new life together.

I share this also because my own kids will testify that I have not been a perfect father. I have had to learn some hard things along the way. I have had to ask for forgiveness from my little ones time and time again. I have had to realize that, like my own father, I have a lot of good and bad in me.

I learned from my relationship with my dad how much sons long for a closeness with their fathers. Even now after I come in from a difficult workout, sweating like a pig—and, I suppose, smelling like one—my son Michael will come up to me and say, "You smell great." Although I don't quite believe his words, I understand his longing for closeness with his dad.

The fact is, we can either help and heal our children, or hurt them with wounds which never seem to heal. Our culture is filled with millions of sons and daughters pathetically seeking the affection their fathers never gave them. There are countless sons who were denied any type of intimacy with their dads and now search for it in all the wrong places.

We dads have so many opportunities to do good or evil throughout our lives. I find that incredibly empowering. Regardless of my age and issues, I will always, until my last breath, have an opportunity to connect with my loved ones. Until my heavenly Father takes me to His eternal home, He gives me countless opportunities to do good to my children.

Today, one of the greatest privileges is to have my little ones sit on my lap as I rock them and read to them. I can't express the joy and closeness I get out of stroking the hair of my children, smelling them, and telling them I love them. Men need to be tender. We are never manlier than when we are tender with one another, our kids, or spouses—whether holding a baby in our arms, loving our grade-schooler or hugging our twelve year-old son.

It is also important that men demonstrate love to their wives. Kids love it when they watch Mommy and Daddy showing love to each other. A child needs to know that Mom and Dad are lovers, quite apart from their relationship to him. And it is the father's responsibility to make the child know that he is deeply in love with the child's mother. There is no good reason why all the evidence of affection should be hidden or carried on in secret. A child who grows up with the realization that his parents are lovers has a wonderful basis of stability.

Dads also need to be tender. Becoming a father does not mean merely having someone else's birth certificate in your drawer. Fatherhood is a state of mind—a potentially new and exciting experience. Most men have never played with dolls, fed infants, or played with them for more than a few minutes at a time; most of us have never ministered to the sick, the dying, the physically dependent. We have never explored the vast territory of tenderness and care. Being a dad offers an opportunity that we have never had before and, once our kids are grown, may never have again.

One can't help but wonder how differently some of our fathers might act if they had ever spent time caring for their children—not visiting them to "baby-sit" them, but cleaning, feeding, dressing, and loving them. Instead, many dads are cut off from their children, both by personal fears and by our culture's mores. We lose touch with life's beginnings and our own. It requires almost an act of rebellion for men to discover—and to admit—that our children can reveal to us a new level of loving, something we have been able to share with them that we hadn't allowed with anyone else.

The Good News

The good news is our culture is changing. More men today are becoming involved in the lives of their children. Fatherhood is moving back from the periphery to the center of many men's lives. The word *nurturance* is being liberated from psychology textbooks and permitted to roam in daily conversations.

The real good news is that God is our heavenly Father. In Christ, we know what fathers are and can be. In Christ, we see the divine Father who loves His children even unto death. Earthly fathers need their heavenly Father who has forgiven us our sins, and enables us to forgive our fathers for their and our mistakes. Our heavenly Father has accepted us and, in His beloved Son, enables us to accept one another as well. Our heavenly Father has called each of us by name in Baptism, and enables us to reach out in tenderness, love, and compassion to our children. Christ enables men who have been hurt by absent fathers to learn how to overcome the anger, bitterness, and resentment they have harbored. Christ gives men a graciousness that enables us to love our children and to forgive our dads for any mistakes and sins.

When we dads set our eyes on our heavenly Father, He reminds us how important we are to the well-being of our own sons and daughters. As we recognize that Jesus accepts us and loves us as we are, so too we can accept and love our children as they are. And as our attention is directed toward Christ, we can see that it is never too late to do those things that make a difference in this life. Regardless of our age, it is never too late to "put first things first." It is still possible for fathers and sons of all sizes, shapes, and ages to reconnect and love one another. Like our heavenly Father, who announced at the baptism of His Son, "This is My beloved Son in whom I am well pleased," we dads can say to our sons, "In you, I am well pleased."

UNDERSTANDING & RESPONDING TO THE DIFFERENCES BETWEEN MEN & WOMEN

From the get-go, Dorothy, the Scarecrow the Tin Man, and the Cowardly Lion had to learn to get along. They experienced external obstacles, and they also had personal struggles. They had to learn to walk together, talk together, work together. This is precisely the case in male/female relationships today. Our differences are drastic and we need to learn to identify, appreciate, and work with those differences.

> *Picture this: In the beginning, it's all hearts and flowers, romance and fascination. Two strangers meet, quite unlikely, but as if it were meant to be. The attraction is so strong; it is not difficult to believe that fate had a hand in the arrangements. Eyes play hide-and-seek; hands touch, first shyly and then in firm caress; words intertwine, making a helix of conversation; flesh wends its way into flesh, releasing the DNA of passion that melds two bodies into one. Separate individuals blend their essential unguents and, in the heat of pleasure, the alchemical bond is forged—I and thou become we.*

And, for a time, we are spellbound. We are fascinated with each other. I listen to your stories with rapt attention. You laugh at my jokes, too much. Each touch is electric. We share secrets, take forays and then expeditions into each other's erogenous zones. Gradually the breathless novelty with its mingled fear and desire mellow into comfort. From the warp and woof of diverse histories we weave a tapestry, a shared life.

Then comes the fall. Repetition destroys romance. In the harsh light of day-by-day proximity, the illusion begins to fade. The facades fall away. The same old games reemerge. The gentleman turns chauvinist and expects to be obeyed. The fair maiden is passive-dependent, her magnolia heart conceals a manipulative will. We look at each other across the breakfast table and are locked into our mutual disappointment.

She doesn't turn me on anymore.
He never talks to me anymore, never shares his feelings.

Silently, each swallows the bitter, broken dreams and sinks into disillusionment, routine, habit.

It is precisely at this juncture that many men are in trouble. They become disenchanted with their partner and begin to wander and wonder about other women. Instead of dealing with their own boredom and anxiety, men will cast a furtive glance at other women in the hope that "maybe with that person I can find the happiness I so long for." In recent years, marriage, fidelity, and the nuclear family have been subjected to a lot of bad-mouthing. The suspicion grows that monogamy produces monotony. TV and the movies sell us the ideal of glamorous romance and then give us an Archie Bunker view of marriage. No wonder we joke, "Marriage is a fine institution. But who wants to be committed to an institution?"

The current focus on personal happiness and personal growth and the right to experience everything have led many men to the conclusion that confinement within a single relationship or in a family may be hazardous to one's personal well-being.

The Disillusionment with Marriage

Of course, our rhetoric and our actions don't match. Marriage is dishonored primarily in our practice, not in our preaching. By middle age, ninety-four percent of adults in our culture have been married. Eighty percent of those who divorce remarry within five years. Sadly, as a culture we have not discovered any effective way to celebrate, renew and discover ongoing excitement in those forms of intimacy we have decided to practice.

A large part of the problem for men comes from the way we think about relationships. The romantic myth, dripping with drama and the promise of constant agony and ecstasy, does not teach us how love actually grows slowly as revelation deepens. It doesn't teach us how honesty grows out of struggle and respect out of fidelity to chosen bonds. The romantic view of love sets up a false dichotomy and forces us to choose between devilish intoxication with constant chance and the deep, blue, depressing sea of matrimony. After all, which of the following columns sounds better to you?

Romance	*Marriage*
Freedom	*Fidelity*
Adventure	*Security*
Excitement	*Comfort*
Novelty	*Intimacy*
Liberation	*Captivity*
Individuality	*Compromise*
Passion	*Family*
Intensity	*Boredom*

When our erotic alternatives are forced to goose-step in such artificial dichotomies, we impose a kind of inner fascism on our spirits. The majority of us marry because a life without bonding is too lonely, empty, and comfortless, but we continue to suspect that we may have betrayed ourselves. We think, "Perhaps if I had been a little more together, braver, less dependent, I might have chosen the truly heroic path—riding the crest of each moment, moving from pleasure to pleasure, promising and expecting nothing beyond the fulfillment of the moment. If only I had ruthless courage, I might have avoided entangling alliances and walked away from lovers, jobs, and institutions the moment they became boring."

In fact, our disillusionment with marriage and the current crisis in intimacy are inseparable from all the other social problems emerging in American society. The energy crisis and the intimacy crisis are flip sides of the same coin: our addiction to excitement, movement, action. We must have intensity, change, growth, and progress. We don't hold still long enough to sink roots. Moving as we do (on the average of once every five years), we regularly divorce ourselves from place, neighborhood, and community. I asked an insurance executive who had moved eight times in fifteen years if this limited his friendships to people within his company. "I wouldn't say that," he replied. "I just don't have friends anymore. After awhile it was too painful to say good-bye, so my wife and I just join the appropriate clubs when we move to a community, but we never really get close to anybody." Our habit of divorce from persons and places is the sacrifice we make to the god of perpetual motion. We are in a hurry to be somewhere else. The machine-driven pace of our lives does not allow us the luxury of cultivating friendships, husbanding our intimacies, growing our families, tending our communities.

Marriage and the family have become the scapegoats for our dissatisfaction. When the excitement of romance inevitably dies and we are no longer "turned on," we often conclude that the problem is with our marriage or with the institution of marriage.

The problem for so many men, however, is that marriage can never make them happy because they expect too much from it. Very few people in our world today are happy, vital, and creative all the time. Why should we expect people who have become devitalized to have vital marriages? Of course there is pain and boredom in marriage; there is pain and boredom in life. Marriage is a way adults live together through an entire life, so it will have some of everything the human condition deals out to us. It is unrealistic to think of life or marriage in terms of constant excitement.

The Response to Boredom

One common way many men deal with the loss of excitement and intimacy in their marriage is to engage in extramarital affairs. Perhaps half of the married men in our society have been unfaithful, or will be some day. Infidelity can take various forms—an accidental and uncharacteristic one-night stand; an overwhelming and disorienting passion that offers escape into fantasy from a reality that is coming on too strong; or a comfortably friendly adjunct to a marriage one can't get out of and can't get back into. Either men or women can have such affairs, but an affair seems to provide an escape route for men who are struggling with a variety of issues.

An affair is particularly alluring if the partner is a younger woman, because the man is temporarily assured that he is not over the hill, but is still young enough to believe in his future. His own wife knows him too well and urges him toward the reality of what he has become. Since the new younger woman doesn't know him as well, she can help him play a game of make-believe. She serves a purpose, as she becomes his significant other, reflecting to him an image of the mature power figure he always wanted to be. Though he knows she perpetrates a myth, he loves it.

It is important to note it is the way she makes him feel that attracts him. He doesn't really love her—he is too empty to love anyone. When she no longer serves his purpose, he will drop her and look for somebody else to give him emotional support. Few are so vulnerable to extramarital affairs as men who are experiencing boredom and apathy. It is this boredom that affects so many men and drives them to do things they never would have dreamed they were capable of. And boredom is a man's number one problem.

Unfortunately, boredom is not dramatic like cancer. It appears to be a minor-league demon, gray and anonymous. There is no anti-boredom week, no crusade against tedium, no boredom anonymous, no foundation for the elimination of boredom. But the amorphous blob creeps into the lives of so many men like a giant fungus in a grade-B science fiction movie. It devours our innocent enthusiasm and destroys our dreams. It insinuates itself into any ho-hum corner of our lives that has been prepared by fatigue and meaninglessness. And the plague is mostly invisible because it paralyzes our power of perception even as it invades our souls. So many men suffer from it that they consider it normal, part of the inevitable atmosphere of modern life.

We have learned to accept tedious jobs, depressing cities, deadly bureaucracies, the television wasteland, and hopeless politics as the way things are. Lively people, full of sap and sass, content with simplicity and few things, are rare as authentic Shaker furniture. Wisdom has become an antique virtue, to be studied in the tintypes of great men of former ages. And wonder, which ancient philosophers celebrated as the aim and reward of a good human life, never makes the cover of *Rolling Stone* or *Newsweek*.

The blahs have us. The Sisyphus train. The disease from inner space. Some vampire is quietly sucking away the lifeblood of our enthusiasm and hope—that spirit that former ages called the "soul." Most frightening, we allow our vitality to ebb away with scarcely a protest. Or we decide to do something about it and the quick fix and instant gratification are found in a tryst with another woman.

An Affair of the Heart

Christian men often have sufficient grounding in the teachings of the word of God so as not to become sexually involved outside marriage. However, many men who would never "touch" another woman can become emotionally involved with extramarital partners in ways that can prove to be dehumanizing to their wives, and deceptive to themselves. Time and time again, I have counseled men who have not been sexually unfaithful, but who have allowed women other than their wives to become their "significant others." This is a very common practice even among clergymen, who often find in their congregations attractive women who are escaping from their own empty lives through romantic fantasies. Such arrangements are often clothed in phony nobility, as the partners blasphemously suggest it is their loyalty to Christ that keeps them from going to bed together. In their pretense of Christ-like behavior, they massage each other's egos, at the expense of their respective mates.

It is amazing how cruel Christians can be while pretending to uphold the letter of God's Law. No wonder Jesus pointed out that even if a man did not sleep with a woman, he still may be committing adultery with her in his fantasies.

This escape route leads nowhere. It is only a matter of time before the new arrangement loses its value as an escape from despair. Then the man will have to move on to another affair, as he seeks to buttress his faltering ego. Like Don Juan, he has failed to see that the absence of lasting gratification is not in his sexual partner but in his own inadequacy.

Building Hedges

Some men envy tales of great sexual conquests by other men. We hear of stories about John F. Kennedy having three women at the White House or Warren Beatty having a short romance with every desirable woman in Hollywood. I have known men who have been unfaithful repeatedly to their wives and they seemed to live almost charmed lives. But as time marches on, these men—once envied by other men—have a hard time of it. They have little comfort at home. They have not found love, and they have not found their masculinity. Being unfaithful to their spouses means these men have to be dishonest, and they spend their lives entirely behind enemy lines, hiding and faking it, never really able to relax with someone who knows them.

Men who seek to find themselves by chasing women just lose more and more of the masculinity they are seeking. They sacrifice the wife who could know them and love them, and the children through whom they could know themselves. Like the little brown beagle who chases his tail again and again, these men continually go around in desperate sexual circles, chasing their own tails.

On a very practical level, men need to put hedges around their lives, their marriages, their families, and their sexuality, to safeguard their relationships. Following are some good ways to build hedges as it were, especially for those who work closely with women.

- *Refrain from verbal intimacy with women other than your spouse. Do not bare your heart to another woman, or pour forth your troubles to her. Intimacy is a great need in most people's lives—and talking about personal matters, especially one's problems, can fill a need for intimacy, awakening a desire for more. Many affairs begin in just this way.*
- *Do not touch. Do not treat women with the casual affection you extend to the females in your family. How many tragedies have begun with brotherly or fatherly touches and then sympathetic shoulders! You may even have to run the risk of being wrongly considered "distant" or "cold" by some women.*
- *When you dine or travel with a woman, make it a threesome. This may be awkward, but it will afford an opportunity to explain your rationale, which, more often than not, will incur respect rather than reproach. Many women business associates will even feel more comfortable dealing with you.*
- *Never flirt—even in jest. Flirtation is intrinsically flattering. You may think you are being cute, but it often arouses unrequited desires in another.*
- *Be real about your sexuality. Most men don't take seriously the power of their sexuality. It is possible to fall. It is possible to become sexually attracted to a woman other than your spouse.*

I have asked my students in class, "Do you think you could fall in love with another woman?" Many of the students answer unequivocally, "Never." I then ask, "If you started dating another woman while you were married, do you think you could possibly fall in love with her?" Many answer, "Well, yes, if that happened I could, but that's ridiculous."

I then make it clear that it is possible to fall for another woman if certain hedges aren't in place. Most of us realize it would be improper to date another woman while we are married, so we make that a hedge. We don't date other women. But so many of us forget that other hedges might be necessary in order for us not to fall and go down the path of sin. We must be ruthless when it comes to our own sinfulness and our own capacity for falling into sin. Do not succumb to vain gnostic prattle about your being a Spirit-filled Christian who would never do such a thing. I well remember a man who indignantly thundered that he was beyond such sin. He fell within months. Face the truth—King David fell, and so can we.

Finally, remember who you are. You are the Lord's man. You have been baptized! And in your Baptism, God says, "[You] were therefore buried with [Christ] through baptism into death in order that, just as Christ was raised from the dead through the glory of the Father, [you] too may live a new life" (Romans 6:4). You have been bought with a price. You belong to the Lord Jesus who, in His death and resurrection, has won you to Himself. Because you belong to Him, are loved by Him, you must continually ask yourself, as Joseph did when he was tempted by Pharaoh's wife, "How then could I do such a wicked thing and sin against God?" (Genesis 39:9). And he fled! "Flee the evil desires of youth, and pursue righteousness, faith, love and peace, along with those who call on the Lord out of a pure heart" (2 Timothy 2:22).

Remember Jesus' words, "The One who is in you is greater than the one who is in the world" (1 John 4:4). Despite our culture changes and the rampant emotionalism and drive to find happiness, Jesus has given us something greater. Jesus has given us something that doesn't last only a few moments or days, such as the passing pleasures of sin. Rather He gives us Himself and His kingdom that lasts now and forever. Remember, you are not your own, you were bought with a price.

10 *The Pain-Filled Journey*

IT'S OKAY TO HURT

During the journey to the Emerald City, each of the main characters expressed their pain in a different way. For example, Dorothy yearned for home. She continually expressed her pain, sadness, and grief. She cried. The Cowardly Lion, on the other hand, denied that he even had a problem. He barked and he growled. That was, of course, a cover-up. He was afraid of exposing his vulnerability until Dorothy slapped him on the nose. Sometimes, that's exactly what it takes (metaphorically speaking!) for men to express their pain.

As many other authors have indicated, men speak a different language than women. The language, however, is no less poignant and meaningful than that of women. What men lack in apparent frequency, fluency, and intensity of language, they more than make up for in a unique richness and complexity.

Time and time again, men are accused of lacking emotional depth, and the ability to express themselves fully. In reality, it's not that men don't speak with emotion, but rather that their language is not often acknowledged or validated. This feeling is not unlike what many women feel when they must conform to a predominantly masculine ideal of what is considered competent.

Women enjoy special advantages in the world of communication, both biologically—in terms of greater innate talent in this arena—and culturally, in that they are specifically trained to be sensitive to nuances of feeling. Men, on the other hand, have been told since they were first able to understand language that if they are going to make it in this world, they must do it by hiding what they really feel.

Men do express themselves through a variety of emotions, including tears, even if their communications are ignored, unappreciated, or misunderstood. One reason for this is that men's strongest and deepest emotional expressions are not of pain, but of empathy, pride, and joy. Once you apply an appropriate framework for understanding the unique language that expresses uniquely masculine values, men are found to be remarkably articulate in their feelings.

I am not just talking about the so-called renaissance man who is in touch with his "inner child," nor the sensitive yuppie who participates in male bonding sweat lodges, eats sushi, and has done a lengthy stint in therapy. Almost all men have within them the capacity to speak deeply regarding their emotions if only people knew how to hear them.

What, Me Express Emotion?

Picture this: Four guys are sitting around a table, drinking beer, and talking about their lives. They are overheard presenting their respective opinions about why the local college football team lost its last game. They debate who has the best prospects in the tightening home run race as the season draws to a close. They discuss politics for a while, making fun of the candidates in the next election, finding each one comical and unacceptable. But their laughter ends abruptly as one of the men begins telling his friends about the feelings he had watching his son play tennis in a state tournament.

"I couldn't believe the way my little guy was so self-assured and composed out there. I was so proud of the way he handled himself. I didn't care if he won the match or not—I just couldn't believe what class he showed."

Tears come to the man's eyes as his voice chokes with feeling. His friends are utterly still, riveted by his story, their attention split between what they have just heard and what they are feeling while they relate to this experience in their own personal ways.

One of the men reaches over and affectionately punches his friend on the arm. To an untrained observer, it would appear he is making light of the story, sloughing it off, anxious to move away from the terrain of emotion and tears and back to the familiar ground of politics and football. Make no mistake. He is, instead, profoundly moved by what he has just heard. The presence of his friend's tears speaks to him in a way that makes him feel like crying as well. In fact, to anyone who looks at him closely, it is apparent that he is crying, though no sobs can be heard, and no more than a little extra moisture can be detected along the bottoms of his eyelids. If you look further, you will see the fingernails of his left hand digging into his palm, his eyes blinking rapidly, and his breathing accelerated both in depth and pitch. This man has been moved, after all, not only by his friend's story, but also by feelings of regret that he did not have children of his own and will never know what it feels like to look with pride on a son or daughter.

Here is a man who is crying, perhaps not technically, as no actual tears escape his lids, but on the verge. Likewise, if you look around the table, another of the men is crying in sympathy. Again, tears are not actually visible, but if you looked closely at his trembling lip and nervous foot, or better yet, got inside his head and heart, you would feel the intensity of his reaction.

So, what is it about this episode of restrained tears that qualifies for being included in this book? How can this really be called an emotional experience and expression when the man did everything in his power to keep himself from demonstrating emotion? The answers are, of course, found in the various ways that men are moved and express their feelings.

Masculine Expression

Forms of self-expression can be both obvious and subtle, flamboyant and restrained. One of the reasons men's emotions have gone unacknowledged is because they don't conform to the usual standards we have come to expect from the more dramatic emotional demonstrations characteristic of women.

Specifically related to the distinct language of emotions spoken by men, the following features are most evident.

Men are less inclined to use emotions manipulatively. This is true for the simple reason that such a strategy won't work. Where it is easy to imagine instances in which a woman might resort to an emotional expression, even crying as a way to improve leverage, a man displaying that kind of emotional expression during negotiations would only elicit feelings of disdain and disrespect. More often, when a man cries, it is because something authentic is going on.

Men cry subtly. They cry less often, for shorter duration, and shed fewer tears. They make less noise and draw less attention to themselves. In many cases, they even hide their faces when they are crying, so as to minimize the literal "loss of face." Whereas until puberty boys and girls cry just about as often, even if there are different triggers for these emotional events, there is a dramatic change at about the time boys are expected to adopt the more traditional values of male adults. For example: A young girl playing her first junior high basketball game falls to the floor, grabbing her knee. Tears begin to fall. What do the coach, fellow teammates, players, and the crowd do? They have concern and show compassion. They help the player up and take care of her. Imagine the same scenario with a junior high boy. He falls and grabs his knee and begins to cry. What is the reaction? "Come on, suck it up." "Walk it out'" "Can you play." In fact, I dare say that as much as a young boy may want to cry, something very powerful within him is screaming that whatever he does, he'd better not shed tears or show emotion. Anger, yes. Sadness or pain, no. We create such a double standard where it is permitted for girls to cry and forbidden for boys or men. Why?

Male tears tend to be most uniquely expressed in those situations in which men were designed to function: in combat, either in the battlefield or in simulated conditions. Thus, crying for fallen comrades is especially within the male province.

Men look toward internal rather than external cues when they cry. The male nervous system seems to process information differently than the female nervous system. Male tears arise from altogether different cues, especially those that are internally rather than externally based. Whereas women look more at external cues in the environment and social interactions, men are more inclined to tune in to their bodies. For example, a woman may cry in response to what is being said or done to her; a man is more likely to shed tears as a result of what he is experiencing in his body as a response to what happens in the outside world. First, he watches his child being born. Then he notices that his heart is racing, his stomach feels fluttery his throat is constricted. Then his tears start to flow. The process often requires one more step between an activating event and the subsequent tears.

Men cry most uniquely in response to feelings that are part of their core identity. Just as women are most fluent crying in response to themes of attachment and loss, men specialize in tears related to their basic nature. However, they are conditioned to hold these feelings in check.

Men have a unique identity, one that is framed in most

cultures in the roles of provider, protector, warrior, athlete, husband, father, and team player. There are particular feelings associated with each of these assigned or adopted roles—male tears are more inclined to express felt experiences of pride, bravery loyalty, victory and defeat.

A man cries as he hears himself warn his child to be careful as she leaves the house. Why? Because he remembers his father saying the exact same thing to him. A man is praised by a colleague at work, sparking an unexpected torrent of tears. Why? Because he is deeply appreciative that his extra efforts have been noticed by someone; he is not used to being acknowledged by other men. A baseball player sits in the dugout and cries for fifteen minutes after his team has lost the World Series. Why? To express his deep feelings of disappointment at trying his best when his best wasn't enough. In each of these instances, men cry in a unique response to an event or experience—and in a different way than the average woman would respond.

Men are not inclined to explain their tears, emotional pain, or anguish. Men are not only less willing to do so, but they are far less motivated than women to talk things through. It is as if the tears speak for themselves. Thinking about them diminishes their meaning and power, Men prefer instead an action mode, one that leads to taking care of what is bothersome, or at least putting things far enough behind so business as usual can resume.

While our culture labels such behavior as restrictive, insensitive, inarticulate, and other negative adjectives, most of these judgments are made within a largely feminine definition of communication, which is espoused by most social scientists and mental health professionals. That accounts partially for the disproportionately small number of men who agree to participate in therapy, and for the way those who do are more likely than women to drop out prematurely. As one of my colleagues has pointed out, "When it comes to therapy, we men always get the 'booby' award! We know we will blow it. We know that our wives are one up on us because therapists invariably talk about feelings and women are much more conversant about feelings." The task of therapy is one in which participants are asked—demanded by some therapists—to acknowledge and express feelings in particular ways. Often, this task is inconsistent with what men have been taught all their lives to do. As one male client who had a Ph.D. in engineering said to me, "If you talk about feelings you will lose all credibility with me." Although he might *experience* his emotions, he certainly did not want to talk about them.

As a result, men work hard to suppress and curtail their tears. I remember standing at the casket of a dear friend. I had been his pastor and he was a beloved member of the church. Paul had served as elder, evangelism leader, teacher; he had occupied almost every position in the church at one time or another. He was a great man and a dear friend. I approached the casket with my family. The entire church was filled with family and members of the parish. I remember the inner dialogue I had: "Don't cry. Suck it up! Be a man!" Although on one level I knew it was "okay" to cry to weep over the death of a beloved friend, on a different level, something inside me constrained me to push back the tears, fight the emotions, keep a stiff upper lip. I was amazed at the anxiety I felt at that moment. I was incredibly surprised at how my socialization manifested itself even at such a critical moment. I had been taught to stop the tears from flowing. I had learned there is value in my ability to regain control of myself even under the most difficult of situations.

I have also discovered that when men do have an "emotional outburst" we apologize for it. We apologize for our tears because we have never been rewarded for crying. Because such behavior represents a humiliating loss of control, men are likely to feel remorse and shame after letting their feelings show. Rather than feeling good about their authentic expressions of self, or even relieved at the release of tension, they more often feel some degree of regret and resolve to show more self-control in the future. The result of this self-restraint is that the average man cries much less than the average woman.

Culture's Role in the Stereotype

We have been conditioned by our masculine Stereotypes. During times of sadness, for example, girls are encouraged to talk about their feelings, to cry, to support one another through touch and compassionate listening. Boys, on the other hand, are told not to sit around and mope, most definitely not to cry like a baby, but to express themselves through productive work or aggression.

I have noted repeatedly the role our culture has in determining men's behavior. Many men and women have been socialized into a particular way of behaving. Sometimes these behaviors are quite helpful. They help us adjust, get along, function in society. It is not helpful for men to cry every time something painful occurs. It does not aid a man in his self-development to stop everything and "have a good cry" each time he is touched by something. However, it is important to note that our tears, our painful feelings, are still very much gifts from God. I suggest our emotional life, especially our tears, are in one sense God's gifts to us to help us become aware of issues around us and in us. And to our harm, we ignore those God-given messengers.

Prophets' Voices

In Scripture, prophets are noted as "problems" for the communities in which they live. The prophet Jeremiah, for example, was told to speak harsh words to the ruling class of his day. Biblical prophets, we know, delivered a message of criticism and hope in an atmosphere of numbness and death. They proclaimed a God committed to truth, compassion, and justice against a culture that defined God as servant to the status quo. The prophetic message addressed a deadened present with implications for an energized community in the future. The oppressed received the message with amazement; the privileged with resistance. Jesus, in full prophetic tradition, upbraided the use of the Law for status and privilege over and against the original meaning of the Law: living God's will in compassion and forgiveness because the kingdom is truly present in Christ. Jesus' voice and the prophets' voices made people aware of things they had long tried to forget. The prophets helped awaken people from their deadness. God's Word moved in their hearts and the part of them that had been buried, oppressed, and harassed was exposed to the light.

In a way, our painful emotions, even our tears, are prophetic voices for men as well. It is not that they point us to

God—they cannot. Only God and His Holy Word can do that. But these messengers, these emotional prophets can help us become aware of parts of our lives we have buried. As painful as these emotions may be, even as the prophets were "painful" to people who did not want to hear their message; these emotions can jar us awake from our lethargy and point us to issues that must be dealt with. Our emotions, our tears can be a voice both critical and energizing. Like messages from the prophets and from Jesus, these emotional voices disrupt a wearied deadness within us and suggest possibilities for new and vigorous life. But most men are unnerved by their urgency.

As part of my doctoral work in marriage and family therapy, I was required to engage in supervision with my doctoral advisor. It was an incredibly helpful experience. Dr. Jory helped point out my blind spots and raise my awareness of a particular issue. He also served as a mirror to me regarding my own issues. He assisted me greatly in becoming aware of issues that were driving me and might also be impacting my interaction with a client.

At the time, I was seeing a couple who had tremendous conflict. No matter what the wife attempted as a solution, nothing was good enough. Her husband, although saying he was eager to work on the marriage, fought her every step of the way. He was in his mid-fifties. He had been raised in an emotionally distant family. He believed that men should "rule the roost," and never ever be questioned about their decisions. With an attitude like that, it was easy to see why there were so many difficulties. But somehow during the course of therapy, I became stuck. I found it increasingly difficult to confront this angry husband in an appropriate fashion. Having power over his wife, he now gained power over me and I, in a sense, became compliant in his poor treatment of his wife.

During supervision, Dr. Jory made one simple statement to me, which almost brought me to tears. (I say *almost* brought me to tears because, for all I was worth, I was going to fight back the emotions.) I felt myself get overwhelmed by a gush of emotions and I did not want to deal with them, nor was I certain I *could* deal with them. His simple statement to me was this: "Wow, do you have issues with your father." That was it. But he was insightful enough to know that even though "fathering" had never come up in session, much of my reaction to this client was based on my relationship with my father. And suddenly, as if I was fourteen years old again, every memory and emotion came flooding back. But this time, I fought it. I was unnerved by the event. I was not prepared to deal with the onslaught of emotions. In fact, the emotional experience scared me. On one level, I believed I had dealt with any "issues" between my father and me. I thought that at age thirty-four I couldn't possibly have other issues. I also believed that if anybody was "psychologically healthy," it had to be me. I mean, after all, I was a pastor, a licensed therapist, and now completing a doctoral degree in counseling. I couldn't imagine anyone healthier. Little did I realize how much I was hiding from myself, my emotions, my life. Here my emotions were screaming at me to listen to them, to help me become aware of things I had long ago blocked from my awareness. They were friends, knocking on the door of my heart, asking me to pay attention. But because painful emotions are just that—painful—I was unwilling or unable to give them the attention they warranted.

Like many other men, I was unable to receive information from my own feelings, particularly painful ones. Although trained as a theologian, I somehow had been spiritually duped to believe that irritation, anger, or resentment should be ignored. I was taught one must rise above negative feelings. Of course my issue, like many others', is deeper than my conscious efforts to control negative feelings. Intense emotional reactions of any kind threaten to unsettle our understanding of ourselves and take control of our actions. Moms caution their children to "calm down" and, like small children on the verge of a tantrum, we may feel that we will disintegrate, that we must protect ourselves at all costs from the power of these emotions.

Since the beginning of the psychological movement, therapists have concerned themselves with this issue of tightly controlling, indeed blotting out, emotional responses. In my own clinical experience, I have noticed that many men and women ignore a part of their lives that becomes too painful. Emotions threatening to reveal themselves are shut up behind a facade of control. Somehow, instead of God's gifts that give life expression, passion, and warmth, feelings are perceived as the enemy, as something that must be controlled at all costs. But counselors know that feelings, particularly resistant ones, are a significant aspect of human life that we ignore at great cost. Emotional truths remain basic elements in the world of counseling and psychotherapy. Something as ordinary and troubling as our emotional reactions to life may serve as a catalyst for change. They declare, sometimes obscurely and sometimes clearly, but generally with intensity, that something is wrong. They proclaim criticism and hope into a weary personal present.

In one sense, our emotions are like the biblical prophets who spoke out against an accepted reality, a status quo, a tendency to say that everything is all right when it is distinctly not all right. Our emotions are a disruptive voice, one that speaks a truth urgently in the midst of resistance. And that voice is a distinctively uncomfortable one.

Another Voice

Our emotions, then, must be understood as a disruptive element at times, something in ourselves that we may long to silence or ignore. They will be called into action against our will and will threaten the very integration of our understanding of ourselves and our world. They will roar against phoniness in ourselves and in our community. In my situation, my emotions and tears roared out against my own phoniness and my inability to deal with this client. Blaming him as resistant, I was ignoring my emotional life that was redirecting me to my own issues and my own understandings. And, because of Dr. Jory, the emotions would not be silenced. Although I was not particularly pleased with his insight at the time, eventually I came to realize how accurate his assessment was.

Our emotions cry out and threaten us. They do not ask our permission, and they will not be silenced. Like Jeremiah, they cry out against false comfort, "They dress the wound of my people as though it were not serious. 'Peace, peace', they say, when there is no peace" (Jeremiah 8:11). These emotions interfere with our peace of mind, our sleep, our ability to relax after work. They have a quarrel with the world.

Initially, we do not want this voice that begins an urgent quarrel out of love. From our perspective, it does not feel loving so we ignore it at great peril.

There is, however, something even greater crying out to us. God's Holy Word continually reminds us that we are not yet what He would have us be. Life has run amuck. All of us have layers and layers of pain-filled memories that result from sin. Many of us are profoundly burdened with guilt; our lives are framed by deep wrong, by skewed relations beyond resolve. We bury our pain because there is such a heaviness to our lives. And we bury our pain and guilt so we can get on with our lives. And yet this guilt, and sin, must be addressed. It must be addressed by the God who is there, who is real, who Himself has confronted sin in the person of His own Son, Jesus, our Savior. God Himself has noticed our sin. God has not hidden His face from our pain and suffering, but in His own Son, in His broken and bleeding body, God has confronted and resolved our pain-filled lives. God's forgiveness in the death and resurrection of His Son is not a wave of the hand, saying, "After all, boys will be boys." God is angry with sin and cannot stand its presence. God notices the truth about us and He responds to that truth. There is divine wrath, indignation, and anger. Scripture makes it clear that the throne of heaven is filled with rage over our sin. God is offended at the way we have lived.

But because God does not ignore or bury our sin nor our pain-filled lives, He is also able to act, to redeem, to change and transform these lives of ours. God, who Himself is the offended, is the One who gives the ultimate gift of self—the gift of His only begotten Son on our behalf. The very life of God deals with the poison of our sin-filled lives. God's way with us emerges out of His deep love that cannot stand by while we die of the poison. It is God's blood, God's self, God's own life,

God's love, passionately, generously given to us that has dealt with our sin and guilt so we are declared forgiven, righteous in His sight.

This is indeed the wonder of our God and our lives. We who are terrified to even look at our lives have a God who looks, who sees, who notices, and who acts and takes upon Himself our own pain and sin that we might at last be changed. It is, quite frankly, incredible.

11 *No Ordinary God*

A WIZARD BEYOND OUR WILDEST EXPECTATIONS

And finally we come to the Wizard. According to Frank Baum's classic fairy tale, the Great Wizard was not what anyone expected. During the story all we see or hear of the Wizard are his booming voice and his majestic spectacles. We are led to believe that this Wizard is the "all-powerful Oz," who, with a sweep of his hand, can make all things well. But near the end of the tale, Dorothy and her traveling companions make a startling discovery. The Wizard is not really a wizard at all. Rather, he is a small, balding man behind a screen, pulling levers and gadgets to make the great special effects that dupe everyone. Of course, Dorothy and her companions are not only shocked, they are angry—and justifiably so. They had placed their hope in this greatest of wizards only to discover that their trust had been misplaced. He isn't a wizard after all. He is simply a humbug. And, of course, they believe all is lost. But this Wizard, who is not really a wizard at all, is able to perform the most amazing feat. He is able to help each of these characters recognize that what they longed for all along was theirs already.

The Wizard works his wizardry on the Scarecrow, helping him to discover that the brains he so wants are his already. That is precisely why he could figure out ways to get his friends out of the messes in which they always seemed to find themselves. The Wizard reveals to the Tin Man that he has a special heart, which is why his friends had to carry an oilcan to keep him from rusting shut every time his heart was broken. And, of course, the Cowardly Lion, embarrassed at his shadow, is in reality very brave and courageous. He simply didn't know it or see it. He believed he was a disgrace to his uniform. Lions are to be the "kings of the forest." He thought he was a mouse, afraid of his own shadow. But the Wizard helps him discover that courage is not about never being afraid. Rather, courage is the ability to act in spite of our fears and misgivings. The Lion, brave and courageous, fought against the Wicked Witch of the West and, despite his fears, brought back her broomstick. A courageous act indeed.

You see, although a small, balding man, the Wizard in reality had great powers. He helped Dorothy's companions understand that the gifts they longed for—the real gifts of a brain, a heart, and courage—could not be found on a journey. These "gifts" were things they already had. They simply didn't recognize their own uniqueness. They believed that something was missing from their lives. This wizard was truly great because the "magic" he worked was that of understanding the gifts and qualities that can make life special. And it is his "magic" and wizardry the world still longs for and so desperately wants and needs.

Of course, the real "wizard,"—and I hesitate to use that word to describe Him because He is so much more—is our Master, the Lord Jesus Christ. Like Dorothy and her traveling companions, we too discover that He is not what we would have expected.

Much More Than We Expected

There is a well-circulated story about a child wanting to be held by his mother at bedtime. When the mother reminded her little boy that the arms of God would be around him all night, the child replied, "I know, but tonight I need a God with skin on." There is something profound in the child's reply. We all need a God with skin. And although we often recognize the need, we find it difficult to believe that our God, the true God, very God of very God, is just that, a God with skin. In the Old Testament, God's voice is heard in the thunder and seen in the lightning over Sinai. God's voice booms out of the burning bush and out of the mouths of His human prophets. God's is the still, small voice that comes on the soft breeze, saying, "Be still and know that I am God" (Psalm 46:10). St. John, at the beginning of his Gospel, tells us that the very thing we have longed for has now happened—we have a God with skin: "In the beginning was the Word, and the Word was with God, and the Word was God. He was with God in the beginning. Through Him all things were made; without Him nothing was made that has been made. In Him was life, and that life was the light of men. The light shines in the darkness, but the darkness has not understood it. ... The Word became flesh and made His dwelling among us. We have seen His glory the glory of the One and Only, who came from the Father, full of grace and truth" (John 1:1-5, 14).

Although we need a God with skin, most people still have a hard time with the truth that Jesus Christ, who is true God, is fully and completely true man. There are also those who believe that if He were true man, fully and completely, then He is not fully and completely true God. Indeed, He is more than any of us ever expected. In our wildest dreams we never would have come up with a God like this—a God who reveals Himself in a man who grew up and was finally crucified on a Roman cross.

St. Paul, writing to the Philippians, said that Jesus was "found in appearance as a man" (Philippians 2:8). Whatever else Jesus was, He was a man. God the Father declared Him to be the "Son of man." And this "Son of man," is also "the way and the truth and the life" (John 14:6). He who is God is also man.

This is what we mean when we say God is a God-with-us, a God who came to share our lives in solidarity. We do not mean that God solves our problems, shows us the way out of our confusion, or offers answers for our many questions. He might do all of that, but this solidarity lies in the fact that He is willing to enter with us into our problems, confusions, and questions.

That is the surprising good news of God's taking on human flesh. St. Matthew after describing the birth of Jesus, writes: "All this took place to fulfill what the Lord had said through the prophet: 'the virgin will be with child and will give birth to a son, and they will call Him Immanuel'—which means, 'God with us'"(Matthew 1:22-23).

To men who sometimes act like scarecrows, tin men, and cowardly lions, this is incredibly good news. In and through Jesus Christ, we know that God is our God, a God who has experienced our brokenness, who has become sin for us. He has embraced everything human with His tender love and compassion.

What is so wondrous about our God is that He is not someone abstract or distant. His love is real and concrete in His Son, Jesus. In Jesus we see the fullness of God's compassion. For all of us men who cry out from the depths of our brokenness for a hand that will touch us, an arm that can embrace us, lips that will kiss us, a word that speaks to us here and now, and a heart that is not afraid of our fears and tremblings; to us, who feel our own pain as no other human being feels it, has felt it, or ever will feel it and who are always waiting for someone who dares to come close—to us a man has come who truly can say, "I am with you." Jesus Christ, who is God-with-us, has come to us in the freedom of love, not needing to experience our humanity and masculinity, but freely choosing to do so out of love.

Beyond All Understanding

This mystery, this "magic" of God with us in Jesus Christ cannot be grasped. It is so very difficult because if we would have done it our way, our God would have been one of great might and power. If our own "magic" had worked, we would not have a God who hangs dead on a wooden cross. It is so difficult for us to comprehend that we are liberated by someone who became powerless, that we are strengthened by someone who became weak, that we find new hope in someone who divested Himself of all distinctions, and that we find a leader in someone who became a servant. It is beyond our intellectual and emotional grasp. We expect freedom from someone who is not as imprisoned as we are, health from someone who it not as sick as we are, and new directions from someone who is not as lost and confused as we are.

The Wizard of Oz was not the kind of wizard Dorothy and company expected. Our God is not someone we would have expected either. God in Christ reveals Himself in servanthood. The very things that we men so long for—wealth, power, status, prestige accolades—Jesus Himself voluntarily gave up. And Paul points out that He was humbler yet, even to accepting death on a cross. Here the real mystery and power of God is revealed. Not only did He taste fully the dependent and fearful condition of being a man, He also experienced the most despicable and horrifying form of death—death on a cross. Not only did He become a man, He became man in the most dejected and rejected way. Not only did He know human uncertainties and fears, He also experienced the agony, pain, and total degradation of the bloody torture and death of a convicted criminal. In this humiliation, Jesus lived out the full implications of emptying Himself to be with us in love.

In Christ, we see the price God is willing to pay to love us into life. It is the price of ultimate servanthood, the price of becoming a slave.

What is most shocking to our modern male minds is that the very thing we hold near and dear to our hearts, "upward mobility," is the very thing Jesus rejected. His, rather, is a downward mobility ending up on a cross. This is what shocks us. We cannot ever think about ourselves in terms other than those of an upward pull in which we strive for better lives, higher salaries, and more prestigious positions. Thus, we are stunned by a God who embodies a downward movement. St. Paul said it this way: "For the message of the cross is foolishness to those who are perishing, but to us who are being saved it is the power of God. For it is written: 'I will destroy the wisdom of the wise; the intelligence of the intelligent will frustrate.' Where is the wise man? Where is the scholar? Where is the philosopher of this age? Has not God made foolish the wisdom of the world? ... But God chose foolish things of the world to shame the wise; God chose the weak things of the world to shame the strong. He chose the lowly things of the world and the despised things—and the things that are not—to nullify the things that are, so that no one may boast before Him" (1 Corinthians 1:18-20, 27-29).

He is not what we expected. He is not even what we could have dreamed of. He is a God who is wholly other, but now in Christ, a God who is wholly near. He slipped into our world through the back roads and outlying districts of one of the least important places on earth and, throughout the centuries, has been changing hearts and lives of men and women ever since.

He lived for thirty years among socially insignificant members of a negligible nation—though one with a rich tradition of divine covenant and interaction. He grew up in the home of the carpenter for the little Middle-eastern village of Nazareth. After His foster father, Joseph, died, He became "the man of the house" and helped His mother raise the rest of the family. He was an ordinary workman, a "blue-collar" worker. He did all this to be with us, to be one of us, to arrange for the delivery of His life for us. It is no simple thing to make it possible for human beings, men and women, to receive the eternal kind of life. But Jesus put Himself at our disposal.

Cosmic Significance

And if He were living in the flesh in our cities and communities today like He was back then, He could carry out His mission through most any decent and useful occupation. He could be an accountant, a clerk in a hardware store, a computer repairman, a banker, an editor, a doctor, waiter, teacher, farmer, or construction worker.

If He were to come today, He could very well do what you and I do. He could live in your apartment or house, hold down your job, have your education and life prospects, and live within your family, surroundings, and time. None of this would be the least hindrance to the eternal life that was His by nature and becomes available to us through Him. Our human life, with all its problems, difficulties, and issues is not destroyed by God's life but is fulfilled in it and in it alone.

The great mystery of this wondrous God is that through His Son, Jesus Christ, all of us men with small minds, hearts, and wills can be made new. God dwells among us. The real issues that drive us in this world, that make us do so many crazy things, can be met in the life of God's Son, Jesus. Our very ordinary lives are the places God comes to dwell. In very ordinary ways and through ordinary means, God comes to His people. In water and bread and wine, God is present among us, shaping, molding, transforming us.

Apart from God, our ordinary lives are indeed so commonplace that they are of little interest or value. Apart from God, to be ordinary is to be only more of the same. The human being screams against this from his every pore. To be just "another one of those" is deadening agony for us. Indeed, it actually drives some people to their death. But it was never God's intention for anyone.

This is why everyone, male or female, child or adult, wants in some way to be extraordinary, outstanding, making a unique contribution or, if all else fails—wants to be thought so —if only for a brief time. We all long for cosmic significance.

And this amazing God, who gives up His right to significance, honor, power, glory and might, is the One who gives those things to His people. He takes us seriously. He takes our needs seriously. He takes our sin seriously. He steps into our lives and world and, in His death and resurrection, enables us to live differently because we have been made different.

The Wizard of Oz told Dorothy and her friends that the very things they had come searching for were to be had in their own lives—they were within. Jesus Christ proclaimed, not that the kingdom of God is within you, but that it is in your midst in His own person. Because of Jesus, the world in which we live is radically changed. Our lives from the moment of our Baptism on are no longer the same. To Jesus, this is now a God-bathed, God-permeated world. It is a world filled with glorious reality, where He continues to work through His Word and sacraments. It is a world that, because of Jesus, is inconceivably beautiful and marvelous—God is here and God is at work.

No Special Skills Needed

And He is at work for all people. Whether you have climbed the so-called mountain of success and have adopted the masculine stereotype as your script to live by, or simply are plodding along day after day, thinking that nothing miraculous will ever happen to you, Jesus enters our lives and magically, wonderfully, gloriously transforms us all.

If you think back to the Gospels, the people Jesus met with repeatedly were those with no special qualifications or abilities. You would never call on them when "spiritual work" was to be done. There is nothing about them to suggest that the breath of God might move through their lives. They have no charisma, no religious glitter or clout. They don't "know their Bible." They "know not the law" as a later critic of Jesus' work said. They are "mere lay-people," who at best can fill a pew or perhaps an offering plate. No one calls on them to lead a service or even to lead in prayer, and they might faint if anyone did.

They are the first ones to tell you they “really can’t make heads or tails of religion." They walk by us in the hundreds and thousands every day. They would be the last to say they have any claim whatsoever on God. Thc pages of the Gospels are cluttered with such people. And yet, "He touched me.” The heavens have come down upon their lives through Jesus. And they too are blessed—healed of body, mind, and spirit—in the hand of God.

And so are we. In Baptism, quite literally, God Himself touches His people. All of us men who are so spiritually impoverished become blessed because Jesus graciously touches us. The message of God is this: God's presence, His grace, love, mercy and forgiveness are gifts to all in His Son, Jesus. From a human point of view all of us who are regarded as most hopeless, most beyond all possibility of God's blessing or even interest, are now touched by God and declared to be His most holy, forgiven, blessed people. No one is excluded from being blessed.

Slow to Respond

It takes a while to sink in, doesn't it? It is so difficult to imagine that I am loved simply because my lover is head over heels in love with me. It is crazy to think that God can somehow take a messed-up life like mine and change it and make "all things new." Humanly speaking, it is absurd to believe that all people, regardless of their lives and what they have done or not done with them, can be made brand-new. We just don't get it.

But then neither did the disciples. In the Gospels, Jesus proclaims the good news of the kingdom, announcing life and salvation for all people. He brings life where before there was only death. He proclaims that not only are sins forgiven by His death and resurrection, but even life as we know it is now different because God is among us. We are literally new people. But the disciples just didn't get it. In fact, throughout the Gospels Jesus says to His disciples, "Are you yet without understanding?" (See Mark 8:21.) Today we would say, "Hellllllooooo! Anyone home?"

The apostles had their own idea of what life in the kingdom was all about. Very much like men today, they believed in power, might, rules, and rights. I suspect their hopes were largely grounded in material things: a fleet of boats full of fish, a full stomach, and a full purse. No doubt they had their own plans for security and happiness, some less realistic than others. But with a little luck, a calm sea, and a couple of good seasons, they would have it made. They would be able to set up their children and sit back with their pipes and sandals to enjoy a little luxury as the shadows of their lives lengthened. Then into their lives came Jesus, shattering their worldly hopes and restructuring their self-centered dreams.

Although they did get up immediately and follow Jesus, leaving their boats and nets, they did not leave their dreams, their plans, their formulas for success with any notable eagerness. They had their own ideas and expectations regarding the good life.

Why were the apostles so slow to respond? Why are you and I, who are so much like the apostles, so reluctant to give up our old way of seeing things in order to take as our own the divine perspective Jesus gives? We know the vision we have, and we know what life is like with our present vision. We are not sure what would happen to us if we were to give up our old vision. Where would Jesus lead us? What would He ask of us? Perhaps deep down inside we are not yet ready to believe that His will for us is indeed good. Perhaps we are not yet ready to believe that He is the onc who has performed and will continue to perform miracles in the rives of people around the world. We know that He did it for the disciples long ago—but that was then.

The greatest "magic" of all, however, is that God works His grace into our lives even when we don't deserve it or expect it. Only God can make a person a believer. Only by believing in Jesus Christ and His death and resurrection are we men given new brains, hearts, and courage. It doesn't make sense. Faith is not and never has been a matter of intelligence or logical ability.

Unlike *The Wizard of Oz*, however, this is no fairy tale. This is more real than anything you and I have ever experienced. God, in His holy Word, in holy Baptism, in the holy Supper has touched us, and we are never, ever the same. We too are given our hearts' desires—peace and life with God, now and forever.

12 *And the Journey Continues*

MAKING THE MOST OF THE MOMENT

It seems to me

that the mythical story of *The Wizard of Oz* is played out continually in our lives. But if you recall, we never know what happens to the characters once they receive their gifts. Dorothy heads for home, repeating to herself, "There's no place like home, there's no place like home." The Tin Man, Scarecrow and Cowardly Lion are, well, I suppose, left to themselves to make something of their lives. They are left in the Land of Oz to make a difference, I suppose—to think, to feel, to be courageous. If you recall, the Wizard flies away in his great balloon and leaves these three to run the show. But we never get details about what "running the show" is like. We simply trust that their gifts will be used in service to others until the Wizard one day returns.

Something very similar has taken place in our lives as well. When Jesus ascended into heaven, the disciples stood there gazing up and, I suppose, wondering what was to become of them. But the angels reassured them and us that "This same Jesus, who has been taken from you into heaven, will come back in the same way you have seen Him go into heaven" (Acts

1:11). And although He ascended, He has sent us the Holy Spirit to continue His work among us in our hearts, our lives, our homes. But He doesn't give us specific details about what we should now do with our lives. He simply says, "You are in the kingdom, now live as my redeemed, ransomed people." He has sent us the Holy Spirit who comes to us in Word and sacrament and He tells us to remain watchful because we don't know the day or the hour when the Son of man will return. And so we wait.

But as we wait for His grand return, the journey does continue. So many things await us now that we have faced many of the struggles all men must go through. So many thrilling adventures await us as God continues to bless us with His presence and His gifts. The gifts He has given us are meant to be used. We are called into service. We are called to love. Like the Creator Himself, we are called to create something new. We too are left in this world to bring life to others. In the midst of a chaotic world, a world hell-bent on destroying itself, God has left His special gifts behind, you and me.

Called to Be Visionary

And God is not silly to do so. God sees all that He has made, and it is very good. It is good because He sees it as good. God's vision is not a response to beauty, it is beauty's cause. In our own small way, we too create by our seeing, as we can sometimes discover in our moments of artistic creativity. The painter does not merely see and record a scene of beauty, he creates it. What he has seen is enriched by his seeing, it comes into its own in his vision of it.

Likewise, the man of God is the artist in creation, the

poet, the painter, the musician; and he knows this, he discovers his vocation in the world, when he comes to be haunted by a vision, a vision he has to express, but which continually eludes his grasp. He has glimpsed something and it allows him no peace. His only peace is in pursuing it. This is why artists are proverbially poor; their vision distracts them from prospering and becoming rich. And artists are also vulnerable: their vision distracts them from protecting themselves. To be seen is to be wide open, to be hopelessly undefended. And the artist, though he may be furiously angry at times, with himself and with everything else, is surely, in the end, a man who simply cannot condemn. His business is to look, not to judge.

I am not saying that all Christian men should drop everything, and become artists, painters, and poets. Most of us do not have the talent to paint or write poetry or compose music. Most poems written by novices are atrocious—including mine. But we are called to something not unlike the artist's way of life; to be haunted by something that will not let us go, to be dragged, almost unwillingly at times in quest of a vision we have glimpsed. Because of this we must—we cannot help ourselves—take one more look at things, in case, in case ...

We may be prudent men, able to make all kinds of calculations, but what we have seen cannot be confined within prudence and calculation. There is a power of life, of light, of beauty, of truth, welling up within us and almost forcing us to surrender ourselves to it, to become its vehicle of expression.

The Author of Our Lives

Peter said that "We are eyewitnesses of His majesty" (2 Peter 1:16). So we are in one sense. We have witnessed the great God who comes to us in very ordinary ways and means. The mighty God has taken on our flesh and bone and blood. He came to us in the simple waters of Baptism, which are no longer simple because they are connected to the Word of God. In the ordinary elements of bread and wine, we partake of the very real body and blood of the Lord Jesus Christ. Indeed we too have seen and are never the samc. But most important, we have been seen. We have been seen by God and we have been loved by Him. Life, whatever it was, is no longer the same. The story of our lives, regardless of the many male myths we adopt, is now written by the Lord of life Himself.

Transformations really do occur and spells can be broken. Dorothy and her companions came out of the "spells" they were under by recognizing the gifts that were already theirs. A great "magic" was required to liberate us from who we were—not just men who have bought into a masculine script, but men who were lost in our own sinfulness.

But I also realize that some men who read this might say to themselves, "Humbug. Sure I have my issues, my 'masculine myths' play themselves out in me—so what? Who doesn't? Besides, I'm not sure I even want to change."

There are hidden advantages to continuing to live within the myth, even when it has outlived its usefulness. By remaining loyal to our pasts, we deny that our precious time and energy have been wasted and our selves betrayed. Moreover, there is some consolation in the belief that what was and what is simply had to be, and there is some pleasure in throwing up our hands and saying, "This is the way I am. I was this way in the beginning, am now and ever shall be, world without end." We shrug our shoulders and declare, "Well, that's just the way I am and I can't do much about it." However, this method of dealing with our issues has its obvious limitations. As long as we continue the deception and insist it is no deception at all because this "character" is who we really are, we do not undo the damage done us, but only rename it so we can live more comfortably with it.

As some men continue their journey, they live stubbornly with their mythic selves, refusing to change. Others, however, blame everyone else for their lot in life and accuse parents and family members for their problems. They condemn the past, yet at the same time hold onto it by blaming it for their present problems and anxieties. It may feel good to point the finger, but it becomes a dead-end street. By blaming culture, parents, church, and school for our present problems we take on the role of victim. And then we are forever tied to our supposed victimizers. The spell is still cast and we remain forever the same.

Rewriting the Script

The masculine script does help some men shield themselves from the truth about themselves and the truth about people in general. We think we can do it all and maintain a facade of control in our lives and in the world. But we are sadly mistaken. When the mythic shell begins to crack and we come to terms with our limits, our own finitude, our own selves, we can become quite fearful.

As we become aware of our assumptions and the various myths that have scripted our lives, it is possible to rewrite the script. We do not have to allow our lives to be trivialized by any script other than the one written for us by the divine hand. As we also face our struggles and issues—whatever they may be—we can begin to see that we have been passive onlookers in our own lives. But now in Christ, God who has called us to Himself, hands us the pen and says, "Here, you continue the story." Write a 'gospel story' with your own life.

As we begin to revise and edit the story of our lives and our distorted images of ourselves, we also seek confirmation and support from others. We all wish at some level to share our discoveries with those closest to us and, in the process, reassure ourselves that our journey out of the world of the masculine myth is not a solitary one. But we must remember that we may not immediately find the responses we are looking for, as our parents, siblings, friends, mates, and children find it hard to figure out just who we are. They also have their own mental picture of men and to change it may take some doing. But it is worth doing.

Watch the surprise in your kids' faces as the dad who never shed tears, never showed emotion, never hugged or spent time belly laughing, begins to do all of those things and more. Watch with delight as relationships are changed as people encounter the real you for the first time. No longer playing a role that you didn't want in the first place, you begin to give yourself authentically to others. You go outside yourself, transcend yourself, and make real connections with others. Here people meet a real man who can be strong when necessary but who can also be vulnerable. No more role-playing. No more keeping people at a distance. No more fake and shallow relationships.

It will take some getting used to. Not only for the man who changes but also for the people in his life. But the depth and reality of these new relationships makes everything else pale in comparison. I still get strange looks from some family members to whom I give a great big hug when I say hello or goodbye. They aren't used to it and neither am I, but I believe the effort is worth it. We are so used to keeping people at a distance, physically and emotionally. The handshake will do, we suppose. And it might for some people. But for me and maybe for you, life depends on our taking those little risks that make it worth living. Give yourself over to the need for intimacy, love, and closeness. Break free from the old forms that have narrowed and restricted your life. Challenge your old masculine script and move away from your comfort zone.

Although there is never any guarantee that other people will agree to see us as we are, and surely no guarantee that they will prefer us to our old masculine selves, we can certainly make it clear that we are taking off our various costumes and getting down from the stage so we can live out, not *act* out, the rest of our lives. When we do this, we may actually inspire others to follow and do the same.

Presiding over this whole business of change and transformation stands the cross of Christ. There we see man tested to the very limit and not wavering in love or fidelity. On the cross of Christ the testing of God's people finally discloses a human response that is wholly true. And it is broken open that we may share it. There we find the God who, with His mind, heart, and will, gives Himself wholly into our humanity because He knew that, left to ourselves, we would be lost.

But here is also the ultimate test of God's love. His is a love that has demonstrated it does not flinch even when we do our worst. It is a love that is courageous, and can absorb all our sins and deep-seated pathologies. As Matthew says, "He took up our infirmities and carried our diseases" (Matthew 8:17).

Jesus in the Here and Now

The cross of Jesus confronts us both with God's supreme consolation: "Whatever you are, I can love you;" and with the hammer of the Law: "This is what you do to love, this is what you are really like." In acknowledging God's love for us, we must also accept the judgment of that insult. Love, in our broken world of sin, can never be other than forgiveness.

And those men who are prepared to accept that all-forgiving love, are at once caught up in the grandest journey of all. We are making our way toward heaven—our own Emerald City of sorts. And on the journey we have a task of declaring God's love to the world. But it is not simply information. Those who speak God's Word of love are drawn into it themselves, and become vehicles for it. The Holy Spirit, who enables us to speak it, makes us also able to love with the same love shown on the cross.

God's love is not simply a cliché written on signs displayed in football stadiums where it means absolutely nothing. Rather, God's love is explosive. And His love is so powerful, it is quite impossible to take it all in stride. We men are being forged into the kind of people He wants. And this process involves a lot of banging and puffing and burning and cutting. We and all those around us will be caught up in many strange adventures before the journey is done. And in these adventures, we at times hurt ourselves and others. Although made new, we nevertheless still have the old man in us and the old man loves the myths of sin and corruption.

But it is in the everyday hurly-burly of life that the love of God is lived out among us. In the ordinary details of our complicated lives, we now live differently. Despite the effects of a culture that has socialized men into a particular way of functioning, the new life in Christ is lived out in actuality. The Gospel is more than a ticket into heaven, a passport into the mansions of glory. The Gospel means all things are new. *All* things are new—not just some things and some people. We have been invited to make a pilgrimage into the very heart of God.

But too many men believe that the life Jesus gives is meant only for the hereafter—the sweet by-and-by. Too many people use the Gospel as if it's good enough to get them to heaven but not relevant enough to include God in the course of their daily existence.

Does believing in Jesus only enable me to "make the cut" when I die? Or tell me how to vote in the next election? Or where to stand on political issues? Has Jesus been relegated to another time and dimension that quite honestly has nothing to do with where I am in the here and now?

Although those questions are enough for another book, let me simply suggest that they address another myth, more powerful than any masculine myth developed by culture. It is a myth that somehow separates what Jesus does from who I am. It acknowledges that God in Christ declares me righteous but doesn't do a whole lot about making a difference in how this life is lived out now.

He comes where we are, and He brings us the life we hunger for. John said, "In Him was life, and that life was the light of men" (John 1:4). To be the light of life, and to deliver God's life to men where they are and as they are, is the great gift of the Gospel. Suddenly, we have a new way of looking at the world, ourselves, others, and life. He touched me and everything is different.

And because He comes where we are, it is not unreasonable for us to expect that life is now completely different. With our wives, life is magical. Where before there may have been self-centeredness and a desire to have it our way, we now long to give ourselves and our love to our spouses. There is never a concern about who gives more or less. Keeping score is the old way of doing things. Keeping tabs on who gave in the last time there was a fight is simply a reminder that the old man, although dead, has a hard time going down.

Because we live in the kingdom, we are enabled to live differently, to live kindly, gently, compassionately toward others. All the masculine cover-ups and masks that kept us from relating can be removed. We can now give up clinging to our masculine distinctions as sources of our identity, and be taken up into the love of God. We now receive a new self, a new identity, which depends not on what we can achieve, but on what we are willing to receive. This new self is our participation in the divine life in and through Christ. Jesus says we belong to God even as He belongs to God. He says we are children of God even as He is a child of God. He wants us to let go of the old life, which is so full of fears and doubts, and to receive the new life, the life of God Himself. In and through Christ, we receive a new identity that enables us to say, "I am not the stereotypical male. I am not bigger or better based on what I do or don't do. I am, simply put, loved by God."

This new self makes a new life possible. We are lifted out of our competitive natures. Our identity is created through the

Giver of Life and that means I no longer have to base my worth on what others think. Freed from the need to control and have power over others, I can now relate to them. I can go out of myself and my fears and actually engage the people who have been given to me to love.

This is the way of Jesus and the way to which He calls men to be His disciples. Be aware, however, that at first, this frightens most men, or at least embarrasses them. The masculine myths of strength, power, and competition die slowly. Who wants to be humble? Who wants to be last? Who wants to be like a powerless child? Who desires to lose his life, to be poor, mourning, and hungry? All this appears to be against our natural inclinations. But once we come to see that Jesus reveals to us the very heart of God, we begin to understand that to follow Him is to participate in the ongoing life of God. By setting out with Jesus on our journey, we become people in whose lives the very presence of God in this world can be made manifest.

But this is not drudgery. This is not some formidable task that has to be accomplished in the name of God. There is, in a sense, the absolute, complete joy of living a new life and knowing that it really is possible to be different. As one of my dear friends, Rev. Roger Kilponen, says, "Life in Christ is a hoot!" And it is indeed that. We really can jump for joy. This life of ours, sharing God's peace and love with those around us, draws us more deeply into the truth of what we are as God's children.

If life is a hoot, it is because, in spite of everything, we discover the fountain of life bubbling up within us. The truth will set us free. Our Lord said the truth of what we are will set us free from our stiffness and our competitiveness. And this overflowing, cascading gift of life is at times unpredictable. We are never sure how this great joy of the forgiveness He has won for us will manifest itself. Maybe it will be by spending time alone with our thoughts and emotions. Maybe it will be doing the courageous thing, like staying put even when we feel like leaving. Maybe we will have to think about our lives differently, seeing them from a holy and divine perspective. Maybe we will click our heels and grab our wives and kids and sing together of the life that is ours because Jesus is ours. Maybe we can give ourselves over to an intimate way of life. We can give ourselves to others and receive from others without exploitation. "I don't want to use you, I want to love you. I want to experience you. I want to know you. I want to smell you. I want to feel you. I want to grow with you. I want to dance with you, cry with you, smile with you, and laugh with you." These are the things that are now different because who we are is wrapped up in the love of God in Christ.

We are, after all, on our way to the Emerald City. Before long, we too shall see the celestial gates and hear angelic voices. Many have gone before us and many will follow. But the God who was there at the beginning of my journey in the waters of Baptism, will be the same God who is with me as I cross over more treacherous waters—the river Jordan. As I approach the waters of my own death, as the journey will one day come to a close, I need not fear, for the God who has known me for these many years is the same God who will say to me, "Well done, thou good and faithful servant ... enter ... the joy of thy Lord," (Matthew 25:21 KJV). My journey, like that all other believers in Christ, will bring me to my final home.

And so the journey continues. God made us His apprentices and we have learned that we have an undying life with a future as good and as large as God Himself. The journey we have made with Him during this life fills us with anticipation of a future so full of beauty and goodness and grace we can hardly imagine. The Emerald City indeed! We have a celestial city, one made not by human hands, but by our Father's hands, eternal in the heavens.

I must continually remind myself that my life still lies before me. That we are coming to the end of our present journey in this world is of little significance. What matters is that the God who set me on the path is the same God who marks the path with His own body and blood and the same God who will one day welcome me into His eternal mansions.

Until we meet there in heaven, remember that this Lord of life is your Lord. Till we join hands around the throne of God, remember that you are more than you ever dreamt possible. Despite the cultural stereotypes and images many of us have adopted as our own, God is bigger, better, grander. And we are the children of His heart. Remember that. Remember that He loves you and forgives you. Remember that your identity is defined by God and His precious Son, Jesus. Remember that because He first loved you, you are now enabled to love others more profoundly, more magically than you ever imagined. Make love your wager. And as you do, remember, the journey has only just begun. One day, we too will see the city God Himself has prepared for us.

Endnotes

1 William Shakespeare. *Macbeth Vv.*

2 W.D. Howels. *The Rise of Silas Lapham.* (New York, New York: Holt, Rinehart, and Winston, 1957.) Page 58.

3 Marjorie Williams. *The Velveteen Rabbit.* (Philadelphia Pennsylvania: Running Press, 1997.) Pages 13-15.

4 Gaston Bachelard. *The Poetics of Reverie.* (Boston, Massachusetts: Beacon Press, 1969.) Page 12.

5 Mike McManus. *Marriage Savers.* (Grand Rapids, Michigan: Zondervan, 1993.) Page 29.

6 Honoré de Balzac. *Cousin Bette.* (New York, New York: Pantheon Books, 1965.) Pages 214-216.

7 J.R.R. Tolkien. *The Hobbit.* (New York, New York: Ballantine, 1937, 1938, and 1966." Page 200.

8 Lewis B. Smeades. "Controlling the Unpredictable: The Power of Promising." *Christianity Today*. January 21, 1983, pages 16-17.

9 Frederick Buechner. *The Longing for Home.* (San Francisco, California: Harper San Francisco, 1996.) Page 7.

10 Soren Kierkegaard. *Either/Or.* Translated by Steven L. Ross. (New York, New York: Harper and Row, 1986.) Page 18.

11 Viktor Frankl. *Man's Search for Meaning.* (New York, New York: Washington Square Press, 1988.) Pages 16-17.

Bible Verses

In Order of Appearance

INDEX

INDEX

INDEX

INDEX

ABOUT THE AUTHOR

Rev. Dr. Bryan R. Salminen was born in Lansing Michigan. He received the B.A. degree from Concordia Ann Arbor, the M.Div. degree from Concordia Seminary St. Louis Missouri, the M.Ed. degree from Michigan State and the University of Toledo, the Ph.D. degree from St. Louis University. He has also done post-doctoral work at Washington University. He is a licensed professional counselor, a licensed marriage and family therapist and a clinical member of the American Association of Marriage and Family therapy. He served parishes in Ohio and Illinois. He also served as professor of psychology at Concordia University, Ann Arbor and professor of pastoral counseling at Concordia Seminary before serving as pastor at Emmanuel Lutheran, Cadillac Michigan. He has authored numerous articles as well as three books. He has taught in Brazil, Germany, Cambridge England and Latvia. He and his wife Casey are co-founders, developers of Zoe (www.zoescore.com) an on-line premarital counseling program. Dr. Salminen and Casey have three children, Lauren, David and Michael.

More From No Ordinary Men
visit us at www.new-gate.org

AUDIO BOOK

The unabridged version of No Ordinary Men is available on Compact Disc

ISBN: 978-0-9801973-4-1

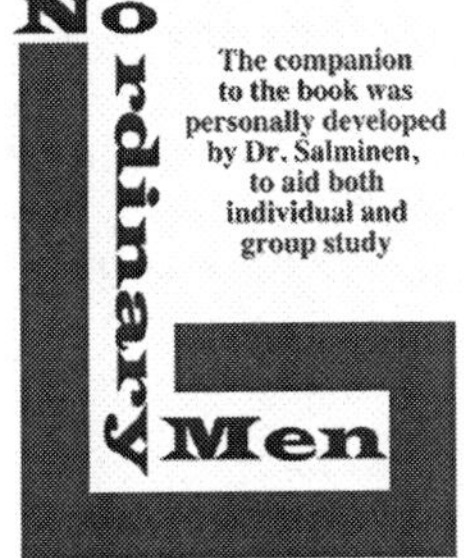

STUDY GUIDE

The complete Study Guide is available as a booklet or digital download.

ISBN: Booklet - 978-0-9801973-3-4
ISBN E-book - 978-0-9801973-5-8

LEADER'S PACKAGE

The comprehensive Leader's Package contains everything a group leader needs to painlessly prepare for either the classroom or a presentation.

ISBN: 978-0-9801973-2-7

Also from Dr. Salminen and New-gate

The Full Contact Rules For The *Christian* Manager

How a 3,000-Year Old Book Can Help You Manage Your Business

Dr. Salminen joins with Brian Keith Jones on this title to consider Christian ethics in modern management. The book takes the unique perspective of grounding each chapter on a single verse of Proverbs, and then analyzing common business behavior through the use of football analogies. A new slant on management that will leave you asking the question, "Why are we doing this?"

Available in trade paperback, e-book, and audio book formats

www.new-gate.org